POOH AND THE MILLENNIUM

By the same author

POOH AND THE PHILOSOPHERS

Pooh
AND THE
Millennium

In Which the Bear of Very Little Brain

Explores the Ancient Mysteries

at the Turn of the Century

JOHN TYERMAN WILLIAMS

With illustrations by Ernest H. Shepard

DUTTON BOOKS • NEW YORK

Library of Congress Cataloging-in-Publication Data

Williams, John Tyerman.
    Pooh and the millennium: in which the bear of very little brain
explores the ancient mysteries at the turn of the century / by John
Tyerman Williams; with illustrations by Ernest H. Shepard.
        p. cm.
    ISBN 0-525-45950-2 (HC)
    1. Milne, A. A. (Alan Alexander), 1882–1956—Characters—Winnie-
the-Pooh. 2. Children's stories, English—History and criticism.
3. Apocalyptic literature—History and criticism.   4. Winnie-the-
Pooh (Fictitious character).   5. Millennialism in literature.
6. Teddy bears in literature.   7. Occultism in literature.
I. Shepard, Ernest H. (Ernest Howard), 1879–1976.   II. Title.
PR6025.I65Z975   1999
823'.912—dc21   98-44162 CIP

Individual copyrights for excerpts and illustrations:
Winnie-the-Pooh, copyright © 1926 by E. P. Dutton & Co., Inc.;
copyright renewal 1954 by A. A. Milne.
The House At Pooh Corner, copyright © 1928 by E. P. Dutton & Co., Inc.;
copyright renewal 1956 by A. A. Milne.

Grateful acknowledgment is made to the Trustees of the Pooh Properties for use
of the quoted material by A. A. Milne and illustrations by Ernest H. Shepard.

Extracts from "Kangaroo" by D. H. Lawrence are quoted
by kind permission of Laurence Pollinger Ltd and the
estate of Frieda Lawrence Ravagli.

Published in the United States 1999 by Dutton Books, a member of Penguin
Putnam Inc., 345 Hudson Street, New York, New York 10014

First published in Great Britain (under the title Pooh and the Ancient Mysteries)
1997 by Methuen, an imprint of Reed International Books, London
First American Edition
2 4 6 8 10 9 7 5 3 1

ACKNOWLEDGMENTS

I wish to thank Geoffrey Strachan, who commissioned this book in the first place, and then gave me the perfect combination of general encouragement and detailed criticism. To Bob Lawrence, I owe the [original] title, the diagram of the Sephirotic Tree, and much valuable assistance from his expert knowledge of the Qabalah. I should also like to acknowledge a lasting debt to the late Tim Lumley-Smith of Lavethan, who first aroused my interest in the Ancient Mysteries. Finally, I am happy to record my good fortune in having as my desk editor Georgina Allen, unremittingly vigilant and the source of many improvements.

CONTENTS

1

POOH AND THE MILLENNIUM

As the Second Millennium of our era approaches, all students of the Great Bear, all true Ursinologists, will expect a major revelation. I am happy to announce that these expectations will not be disappointed. Just as half a millennium ago it was discovered that the universe was physically infinite, so the new age will reveal that the World of Pooh is infinite, spiritually and mentally, equal in esoteric status with such great mythical worlds as Eden, the Golden Age and the Fortunate Isles. A brief glance at the Ancient Mysteries which underlie the superficially childish tales contained in our two texts, *Winnie-the-Pooh* and *The House At Pooh Corner*, should convince the most doubtful.

Think first of astrology. The Great Bear is the best-known constellation in the sky: The very name reminds us of A. A. Milne's Great Bear and alerts us to his astro-

logical significance. Alchemy brings a deeper understanding of Pooh Bear's Pot of Honey, an undoubted
parallel with the alchemist's still, the apparatus used to
transmute base metals into gold. Can anyone look at the
endpapers of *Winnie-the-Pooh* and not notice their
striking emphasis on trees? Can anyone see *that* without thinking of the lore of the ancient Druids? In all
these cases, the connections are so obvious that I have
only the easy though delightful task of expanding and
elaborating the transparent facts. The connections with
some of the other Ancient Mysteries are perhaps more
deeply hidden.

I must apologize in advance to those initiates who
have already passed the Veil and entered the inner
sanctum, but there may be those who do not at once
identify Pooh's pot with the Holy Grail, or see him as a
supreme interpreter of the tarot, a guide through every
process of initiation, a Hermetic Magus, a Noah figure.
Furthermore, even those acquainted with Qabalah—
that great doctrine that underlies all Western occultism—may need to be convinced that Pooh is its
supreme example and expositor. And finally I must confess that, until I set out on this quest myself, I was un-
prepared for the most astonishing revelation of all: that
the apparently masculine society of the Pooh cycle contains, at the deepest level, a revelation of the Female
Mysteries. I think that by the end of this book I shall

have done enough to show that Pooh Bear's knowledge of the Ancient Mysteries does indeed demonstrate not only that his Brain is Enormous but that he is infinite in spirit as well.

How This Small Book Justifies Such Large Claims

After such claims, I have now to map out the course we are to follow and establish it on solid foundations.

Though the World of Pooh may be infinite, this book is not. So it is necessarily selective. This answers a question some readers may ask. They are doubtless well aware of the obvious parallel between A. A. Milne and Dante Alighieri. They will therefore accept that Milne has given us his *Paradiso*, but where, they will ask, are his *Purgatorio* and his *Inferno*? Without them, they may argue, the spiritual universe is surely incomplete. The answer lies in what was clearly Milne's purpose: to prepare us for the Second Millennium. For this he did not need to teach us about infernal evil. That we know only too well. What we are painfully unfamiliar with is a picture of Paradise, with perhaps a reminder of the Purgatory we may need to qualify us for entry. This is what Milne set out to show us, and this is what he achieved.

Let us now return to the coming revelation of Pooh and the Millennium.

The forerunners of this revelation have already appeared. Frederick C. Crews in *The Pooh Perplex* (1963) showed us some of the riches of literary interpretation latent in Milne's great works. Benjamin Hoff in *The Tao of Pooh* (1982) and *The Te of Piglet* (1992) revealed the Taoist wisdom implicit in the Pooh books. In 1995, my own *Pooh and the Philosophers* demonstrated that the Great Bear contains the whole of Western philosophy. Furthermore, considering how many learned works on the Ancient Mysteries were first published in Latin— long the common language of European scholars—it is significant that Latin versions of Milne's original texts (Alexander Lenard's *Winnie Ille Pu* and Brian Staples's *Winnie Ille Pu Semper Ludet*) have been well received.

The reader will notice that these preliminary glimpses of Ursinian truth have followed each other faster and closer as the Millennium approaches. This is precisely what all students of the Ancient Mysteries would expect. Signs and portents cluster as the moment of revelation draws near. Even those less versed in such matters may remember that Shakespeare—himself, as we shall see, a profound master of occult wisdom—tells us how thick and fast the omens came before the death of Caesar. Happily, the signs I am privileged to communicate do not portend disaster but a joyful wisdom.

At this stage, it might be appropriate to emphasize that I claim no personal merit for my role in revealing Pooh as Master of Occult Lore and Supreme Magus of

the Ancient Mysteries. As I studied the profound Milnean texts, I became increasingly aware that powers
greater than mine—dare I say, powers emanating from
the Inner Planes, perhaps from the Astral Spheres?—
were guiding me.

I am also particularly happy to share with my readers two aspects of Ursinian wisdom which hitherto have
been not only unrecognized but distorted, not least
by me.

Readers may well have been surprised by the reference to the Female Mysteries. I must confess I was,
by implication, guilty of a grave omission when I wrote
Pooh and the Philosophers. I did, rightly, deny that the
Milnean opus was racist or speciesist, but I was silent
on the subject of sexism. Now I am delighted to say I
need be silent no longer. The full explanation of Ursin-

ian wisdom in this area must wait until Chapter Ten, but I can say here that, in addition to a much deeper understanding of the role of Kanga, that chapter will explore the significance of several easily overlooked but profoundly indicative examples of gender exchange in the Pooh books.

The second error to which I must plead guilty was in misunderstanding Pooh's relation as teacher or guru to Piglet as his chosen pupil, or *chela.* I cast doubt on Piglet's suitability for this role, and therefore by implication on the correctness of Pooh's choice. Further thoughts, arising from this present work's focus on spiritual guidance, have brought me to see how wisely Pooh led his devoted friend and disciple, step by step, until, at the end, he had become both hero and saint—proving himself a disciple well worthy of his Master's companionship.

My earlier error was caused in part by an excessive concentration on the purely intellectual genius of the Great Bear. This was natural enough in a treatise on his exclusively philosophical aspects, but it should warn us all that no one aspect of Pooh can even begin to exhaust the riches of his wisdom. As true Ursinologists, we must always remember that so far, we have at best made preliminary reconnaissances into a few areas of the illimitable World of Pooh.

Let us remember too that, if ever we read a passage that tempts us to suspect that Pooh is in any way mistaken, experience shows that the mistake is never in Pooh but always in ourselves. Further reflection will eventually convince us of this. I say "eventually" because we may have to wrestle with the text as hard and long as Jacob wrestled with the angel. As with Jacob, courage and determination will, in the end, reward our efforts.

So even these errors to which I have just pleaded guilty should encourage my fellow-students of Pooh to further meditation on the great texts. Let us cherish a humble confidence that such meditation will gradually disperse the mist of error and reveal the light of truth. Pressing forward in this spirit, we may offer our own small contributions to preparing the way for that total Ursinian revelation that will illuminate the completion of the Second Millennium.

Before I present my own offerings in detail, I should like to reassure my readers on one vital matter. Do not fear that my sense of being guided on the path to Pooh's occult wisdom will in any way detract from that commitment to scrupulous scholarship and rigorous logic that readers of *Pooh and the Philosophers* have learned to expect from me.

I think I should also anticipate the question that

must arise in some readers' minds. How, they may reasonably ask, can two short volumes cover the wide and varied range of occult subjects I have mentioned? This is possible only because every incident in the Pooh cycle, every character, every minor reference indeed, is symbol, allegory or metaphor for several different aspects of esoteric wisdom.

Having established a proper confidence between reader and writer, let us now, as far as we are able, follow in the footsteps of Winnie-the-Pooh as guide to the Ancient Mysteries.

How Does Milne Alert Us to the Secret Wisdom in the World of Pooh?

Many attentive readers of A. A. Milne's two great masterpieces have been puzzled by the deeply mysterious references they find in the Introduction to *Winnie-the-Pooh*.

Milne's very first paragraph tells us that Christopher Robin "once had a swan (or the swan had Christopher Robin, I don't know which), and that he used to call this swan Pooh." It is painful to record that not one of my fellow Ursinologists has attempted the plain duty of elucidating this short but challenging passage.

The second paragraph contains a longer and even

more enigmatic reference; not only enigmatic but also disturbing:

> *. . . when Christopher Robin goes to the Zoo, he goes to where the Polar Bears are, and he whispers something to the third keeper from the left, and doors are unlocked, and we wander through dark passages and up steep stairs, until at last we come to the special cage, and the cage is opened, and out trots something brown and furry, and with a happy cry of "Oh, Bear!" Christopher Robin rushes into its arms. Now this bear's name is Winnie, which shows what a good name for bears it is, but the funny thing is that we can't remember whether Winnie is called after Pooh, or Pooh after Winnie. We did know once, but we have forgotten. . . .*

Here, beyond all doubt, we have a passage profoundly problematical, one that demands long and devout meditation from every serious Ursinologist. Yet, so far as my researches have gone, it has hitherto passed without comment. At this stage, we can only make ourselves aware of the problems. The rest of this little book will suggest some solutions for other occult Ursinologists to consider.

First, let us note where Milne has placed this passage: the "Introduction." This clearly implies that it is telling us something essential for our understanding of what follows. Yet most readers, and, I think, all writers, know that Introductions are frequently unread. What are we to make of this? How can we explain that an experienced author, of the highest professional skill, should give his readers essential information in a place where it is likely to be overlooked?

Readers experienced in the Ancient Mysteries will easily understand this paradox. Writers on such subjects typically both exhibit and conceal their mysteries. They conceal them from the superficial, the careless and the hasty. Even to the merely curious, they exhibit them in a form that challenges rather than satisfies curiosity. Only the genuine pilgrim of truth will take up that challenge and seek the path of the initiate. It is to them that this elementary guide is addressed.

I may add that Milne leaves no doubt that his challenge to the enquirer is deliberate. He professes that he does not know whether Christopher Robin had the swan or the swan had him. Even more strangely, he professes that he did once know whether Pooh was called after Winnie or Winnie after him but that he has forgotten. When we reflect that Milne's two Ursinian works show total recall of everything concerning Pooh Bear and his companions, can we really accept such professions of forgetfulness? Surely not. Surely Milne was in fact hinting to us that there was some hidden mystery to which the truly dedicated Ursinologist might devote a lifetime of study.

So far as the swan is concerned, it is mentioned—but certainly not explained—in *When We Were Very Young*. Its true meaning, or one of its true meanings, must wait till Chapter Seven, when its relation with Perceval's swan will be clarified. Similarly, in Chapter Four, the references to the caged bear in the London Zoo will be explained when we meet the great Hermetic philosopher of the Renaissance, Giordano Bruno.

With this in mind, we merely point out that Milne himself has given us a further hint. He tells us that his forgetfulness is "a funny thing." Now fully alert to his occult intentions, we recognize that once again Milne was simply following in the footsteps of the great masters of esoteric truth. He has shown us where to look for the secrets, but to understand them must be our own spiritual quest. His words invite us to lift the veil and peer into the mysteries they conceal. Given this unmistakable invitation, why has it not been taken up years ago? Were all previous readers superficial or obtuse? Perhaps, but another explanation is both more charitable and more specially appropriate to students of the occult: They may have felt bound, as by an implicit vow, to preserve the Master's secrets.

Why then, you may ask, have I now taken it upon myself to be a revealer of secrets, to lay bare the esoteric truths underlying these tales of Pooh and his companions, and to proclaim Winnie-the-Pooh as the Master of the Ancient Mysteries? How can I justify such audacity?

May I remind you that for centuries the Qabalah was a completely secret teaching, handed down by word of mouth from Magus to carefully chosen disciple? Not until the second century A.D. was the *Sepher Yetzirah* committed to writing. The complete *Zohar* had to wait till 1290. Printed editions appeared in the sixteenth century. Why publication of the Qabalah came when it did is obscure. But there is no doubt why the esotery of the Milnean opus should appear now: It is blindingly obvious that this of all times in human history is the destined moment to reveal Winnie-the-Pooh as the Supreme Magus of the Second Millennium.

2

POOH AND ASTROLOGY

How Does Milne Alert Us to the Astrological Aspects of Pooh?

What is the best-known constellation in the night sky? Undoubtedly, the one variously called the Plough, Charles's Wain, Arthur's Wain, and—the Great Bear. Who can look at the Great Bear in the heavens and not immediately think of that yet Greater Bear whose wisdom it is our privilege to study?

Alas! Scrupulous scholarship compels me to admit that the vital connection is not universally made. Charity, a quality not always wedded to scrupulous scholarship, may excuse this astonishing ignorance. It may plead that the variety of names has often confused the unwary. Many who easily recognize the great northern constellation and who cherish a lifelong affection for

Winnie-the-Pooh may have failed to connect the two, simply because they were brought up to recognize the starry pattern by one of its other names. All these names have their own occult significance for Pooh. So indeed have the Greek and even the Sanskrit names that lie behind our familiar English titles. All this should prepare us to find that our Great Bear's unique position in his world is reflected in the world of astrology. Naturally, this is exactly what we do find.

Those who come to the stellar aspect of the Great Bear later in life need not entirely regret the delay. I myself, having been brought up to speak of the Plough, must confess I did not receive the vital insight till quite recently. Can I believe this was mere accident? Anyone who can believe that can believe Winnie-the-Pooh is not the Supreme Magus of the Second Millennium. Let us dismiss such absurdities and recognize that there are no accidents in the world of the mysteries we are now exploring. How frustrating it is that lack of information prevents us from constructing and comparing Pooh's horoscope—if such a construct were possible—with my own! We can, however, rest intuitively confident that those hypothetical horoscopes would show that I, in my study in Tintagel, was destined to make the crucial discovery—just at the right time. Just when I had made sufficient progress to receive the message, and to communicate it when it is most needed—now. Now, when we must all be preparing ourselves for the year two thousand.

Sun Signs and Pooh

Probably most of us have at some time glanced at the "Your Stars for the Week" page in a magazine. We probably know the names of the twelve signs of the zodiac, and our own sign—Taurus, Gemini or whatever. This is our sun sign, the sign of the zodiac where the sun was at the moment of our birth—or of our conception, according to some. Of course, there is much more to astrology than sun signs, but all astrologers agree that these are extremely important indicators of our personality.

Helpful as ever to his truly alert and perceptive readers, Milne has brought the sun and Pooh together near the beginning of Chapter Four of *The House At Pooh Corner*. In case we should miss the astrological significance of this, immediately above the sun reference in the text, E. H. Shepard shows us Pooh sitting on a stone, in the middle of a stream, warming himself in the sun, and clearly contemplating the heavens. To put the meaning beyond all possible doubt, right in the line of Pooh's vision, Shepard has placed a dragonfly. A dragonfly! An unmistakable reference to the constellation Draco (the Dragon), the nearest neighbor to the Great Bear in the northern sky.

Illuminated by this knowledge, we see now what we may have missed before: the clear astrological meaning of Pooh's tree-climbing and balloon ascent in pursuit of honey in Chapter One of *Winnie-the-Pooh*. This incident is too well known to need detailed description here. But it is vital to remember that, in relation to the Mysteries, honey frequently symbolizes truth. We must also remember that astrologically, the tree that Pooh climbs represents the astrologer's observatory. That is, he is seeking truth by ascending toward the heavenly regions. When a bough breaks and he falls to the ground, he comments, "It all comes . . . of liking honey so much." That is, he accepts difficulty and danger in his astrological search for the honey of truth. Undeterred, he tries again, with the aid of a balloon borrowed from the helpful though uncomprehending Christopher Robin. Once again, Pooh seems to be thwarted. He announces that the bees are the wrong sort of bees: A verdict confirmed by the fact that one of them stings him. Eventually he requests that Christopher Robin help him back to earth by shooting down the balloon.

This brief incident dramatizes not only the perils of astrological research, but also of the need—too often forgotten by occultists—to come back to solid earth. Once this is understood, no one will again fall into the absurd but all too common error of supposing that Winnie-the-Pooh was a foolish little bear whose greed led him to a nasty accident, an absurd scheme, and final failure. Instead, they will learn that the most dedicated astrologer must not so lose himself in the heavens that he cannot return safely to earth. This is the lesson that Pooh Bear so strikingly demonstrates. We notice too, not for the last time, his willingness to sacrifice his own safety and dignity for the sake of us, his students.

As we do not know the time, or even the date, of Pooh's birth, we cannot construct his horoscope or even

know his sun sign. We are equally uninformed about his companions. Obviously we cannot cast their horoscopes, and so we cannot reason forward from their sun signs to their characters. But we can perhaps reason backward from their characters to their sun signs. This is admittedly a somewhat hazardous enterprise, and can give only a simplified picture. However, it is worth trying, and I think you will be surprised at how well some of the characters fit certain sun signs. I use the word "fit" advisedly, because modern astrologers tend to regard the connection between heavenly body and person as a matter of synchronicity rather than influence in the traditional sense. That is, they believe that certain human personality traits go together with certain sun signs, and give valuable clues to behavior rather than form it. This belief may have some analogy with Jung's comment "Astrology represents the summation of the psychological knowledge of antiquity."

Let us take a look at a few examples. For the readers' convenience, the relevant birth dates are given in brackets after the first reference to each sun sign.

Tigger

Take Tigger first, a strong, well-defined personality. When they first meet, Pooh asks him,

> *"Do Tiggers like honey?"*
> *"They like everything," said Tigger cheerfully.*

Note: Tigger says that Tiggers like everything, and he says it cheerfully. Next morning, he attacks Pooh's tablecloth.

> *. . . with one loud* Worraworraworraworraworra *he jumped at the end of the tablecloth, pulled it to the*

ground, wrapped himself up in it three times, rolled to
the other end of the room, and, after a terrible struggle,
got his head into the daylight again, and said cheerfully:
"Have I won?"

Even as early as this, we can be sure we are looking at a typical Sagittarian (November 23–December
21).

His assault on Pooh's tablecloth shows him aggressive but still cheerful. Only once does his cheerfulness
desert him. That is when he has bounced Eeyore into
the river. In his embarrassment, he falls short of his normal frankness, incidentally demonstrating the typically
Sagittarian inability to lie convincingly. First he denies
bouncing at all, claiming that he only coughed. Finally
he admits that he "sort of boffed." Such untypical devi-
ousness shows he must have been deeply upset. Soon,
though, he has recovered. As Rabbit says later, "Tiggers
never go on being sad. They get over it with Astonishing
Rapidity." Another typically Sagittarian trait.

When Roo asks if Tiggers can swim, Tigger answers, "Tiggers can do anything." He adds that they can
climb trees better than Pooh: a typically Sagittarian
boast that is soon proved false. He does, however, literally rise to the challenge and climb the tree, with Roo
on his back. It is the descent that exposes his shortcom-
ings. Having nearly reached the top, he discovers he

can't get down, and has to be rescued by Christopher Robin and his friends. Though he exaggerated his climbing abilities, there is no doubt about his physical vigor and love of outdoor activities. Again, these characteristics are typical of Sagittarius.

Indeed, Tigger's vitality is overwhelming. So overwhelming—"bouncy," as his companions call it—that Chapter Seven of *The House At Pooh Corner* is entitled "In Which Tigger Is Unbounced." In fact, however, as all Ursinians will remember, the attempt to unbounce Tigger is a total failure. Rabbit, who has planned the unbouncing, gets hopelessly lost in the Forest, while a quite exceptionally bouncy Tigger "was tearing round the Forest" looking for him.

And at last a very Small and Sorry Rabbit heard him . . . and rushed through the mist at the noise, and it suddenly turned into Tigger; a Friendly Tigger, a Grand Tigger, a Large and Helpful Tigger, a Tigger who bounced . . . in just the beautiful way a Tigger ought to bounce.

"Oh, Tigger, I am glad to see you," cried Rabbit.

Summing up, Tigger is irrepressibly cheerful, full of physical vigor, optimistic and boastful—sometimes mistakenly—often clumsy and tactless, but always forgiven and loved by his companions. Nobody resented his tactlessness for long. We remember how soon the often surly Eeyore forgave Tigger for "boffing" him into the river. Eeyore can hardly have got dry before they "went off together, because Eeyore wanted to tell Tigger How to Win at Poohsticks." Could we have more convincing evidence that Tigger is a Sagittarian?

Rabbit

Rabbit's attempt to unbounce Tigger was a humiliating failure, but the Rabbit we usually see is as confident as Tigger himself. His confidence, however, shows itself in a totally different way, a way that Milne himself describes as "Captainish."

It was going to be one of Rabbit's busy days. As soon as he woke up he felt important, as if everything depended upon him. It was just the day for Organizing Something, or for Writing a Notice Signed Rabbit . . . a Captainish sort of day, when everybody said, "Yes, Rabbit" and "No, Rabbit," and waited until he had told them.

To the astrologically informed Ursinologist, it is obvious that Rabbit is a Leo (July 23–August 22). The passage I have just quoted leaves no room for doubt.

Making plans and imposing them on others is typically Leonine. Rabbit's plan to unbounce Tigger failed, but we remember too that it was Rabbit who planned the kidnapping of Roo, with the purpose of frightening Kanga out of the Forest. This time Rabbit's plan was successful up to a point. Roo was captured, but Kanga knew that no one would really hurt him and so she stayed firm in the Forest.

The deepest meaning of this incident should await revelation until we give our full attention to Kanga in Chapter Ten. Here we are concerned only with identifying Rabbit's sun sign. Leadership is the salient feature, and we are told that a Leo would make a good social organizer. No one would agree more warmly than Rabbit himself. A natural weakness of the Leo character is its tendency to bossiness. It is only fair to redress the balance by reminding ourselves of the equally typical Leonine hospitality. Remember Pooh's "Rabbit means Company, [. . .] and Company means Food and Listening-to-Me-Humming and such like." Even the most skeptical must admit the force of this converging evidence.

Here some readers who have read a little astrology may object that I am being unduly selective. While admitting that Tigger is about as good an astrological fit as we can expect from a sun sign alone, they may well query Rabbit as Leo. The typical Leo, they will point out, is formidable, both physically and psychically. Rabbit is bossy enough, but nobody could call him formidable. He loves organizing others, but we could not call him a consistently successful organizer, nor could we call him a good listener, as a Leo is supposed to be.

On the whole, though, Tigger and Rabbit fit their hypothetical sun signs remarkably well. All astrologers agree that sun signs do reveal a great deal but that they are modified by many other factors. If we had the information needed to construct a horoscope, can we doubt that we should see why Rabbit's plans were so often impracticable? And we should know why Pooh Bear showed his usual wisdom when "he got into a comfortable position for not listening to Rabbit."

Eeyore

I hesitated for a long time in assigning a sun sign to Eeyore. It was finally a consideration of planetary influences that brought me an answer. It was easy to suspect a strong influence of Saturn, but it was only when I consulted Saturn in Virgo (August 23–September 22) that I knew I had found the answer. Seriousness amounting to worry and pessimism, and a lack of self-confidence are typical of this combination: These qualities pointed unmistakably to Eeyore. Further investigation into the typical Virgoan character did not lead to quite such a smooth fit as in Tigger's case, or even Rabbit's, but there was on the whole adequate confirmation. Despite his incarnation as a beast of burden, we could hardly say that Eeyore is the born servant or server of others, as the typical Virgoan is supposed to be. But he is a loner. He is analytical. (Remember when we first meet him, he is thinking about things and asking himself such questions as "Why?" and "Wherefore?" and "Inasmuch as which?") He is highly critical, and occasionally pedantic; as, for example, at the outset of the Expotition to the North Pole. He is prepared to be the end of the Expotition. "But if, every time I want to sit down for a little rest, I have to brush away half a dozen of Rabbit's smaller friends-and-relations first, then this isn't an

Expo—whatever it is—at all, it's simply a Confused Noise." All of these are typical of Virgo, especially when strongly influenced by Saturn.

Piglet

Next to Pooh himself, Piglet is perhaps the best loved of all Milne's characters. So readers will naturally expect to learn something about his place in astrology. I must confess this presents a real difficulty, because Piglet changes and develops far more than any of his friends. At first he is affectionate and lovable but hardly impressive. Yet by the end, he receives the supreme honor of being taken into Pooh Bear's own home. How does astrology accommodate this?

At first glance, none of the sun signs signalled a clear fit. But on further consideration, many characteristics of Cancer (June 22–July 22) did fit Piglet. The typical Cancerian is highly affectionate, with strong

family feelings, impressionable, sensitive, timid. Some of these qualities obviously fit Piglet.

His affectionate nature is stressed from the beginning. He is Pooh's companion more often than any other character. He is always loyal and admiring, even when uncomprehending. Circumstances give him hardly any chance to show the typical Cancerian family feeling; yet it does appear in his frequent references to his grandfather, Trespassers W, and his pride in the fact that this name "had been in the family for a long time." His idea of passing the time with Pooh is to tell him "what his Grandfather Trespassers W had done to Remove Stiffness after Tracking, and how his Grandfather Trespassers W had suffered in his later years from Shortness of Breath."

More importantly, his quasi-filial affection for Pooh is clearly a transference of family feeling. His weaknesses too are Cancerian. He is timid: easily frightened by Woozles, Kanga and Heffalumps. The Heffalump incident shows him highly suggestible but, at that stage, quite unable to understand Pooh. It also displays his extreme sensitivity. When the absurdity of his panic about the "Hoffable Hellerump" is exposed, "he was so ashamed of himself that he ran straight off home and went to bed with a headache."

However, I must admit there are difficulties. The

typical Cancer protects the inner sensitivity with a hard
outer shell. Piglet shows no sign of this. More strikingly,
one of his worst experiences is in Chapter Nine of
Winnie-the-Pooh, "In Which Piglet Is Entirely Surrounded by Water." This is in marked contrast to the
usual Cancer's love of water, a result of the moon's powerful influence on this sign. Clearly, other influences are
at work on Piglet.

Incidentally, while thinking of the moon, it is interesting to note that, though usually female, it is sometimes male in astrology: the first but by no means the
last example of gender-crossing we shall find.

Frustrating lack of data bars us from pointing to the
astrological explanation of the dramatic development that
changes the timid Piglet of the early episodes to the brave
Piglet who "Does a Very Grand Thing," courageously car-
rying out Pooh's plan to rescue Owl and Pooh himself. He
earns the supreme accolade of a special Hum of Pooh's to
celebrate his heroism. Finally he adds "a Noble Thing" to
his "Very Grand Thing" when he sacrifices his own "very
grand house" to the homeless Owl. This time his reward is
even greater: He is invited to share Pooh's dwelling, an invitation that publicly recognizes the formerly somewhat
slow-witted Piglet as the guru's *chela.*

Astrology is only one aspect of the Ursinian Mysteries
we are now exploring, so there is no space to match

more of Pooh's friends with their astrological signs. In any case, it is contrary to all true mystical practice to treat pilgrims on the Way as mere passive recipients of information. It is essential we should make discoveries for ourselves. This freedom I am happy to give you.

What About Pooh Himself?

When we consider the twofold significance of the Great Bear (as constellation and as Winnie-the-Pooh), we are bound to be struck by the obvious parallels. Even those who have hitherto remained blind to the occult wisdom of Pooh Bear, even those who truly believe that he is a Bear of Very Little Brain, must admit that he dominates his world. Milne leaves us in no doubt about this. "Pooh" is the only name that appears in both titles of the great work. While much of the Introduction is profoundly enigmatic, nothing can be plainer than our author's statement "Pooh is the favourite, of course, there's no denying it."

Throughout the work, Pooh Bear's preeminence is repeatedly affirmed. Rabbit may be Captainish, Owl learned and eloquent, Tigger bouncy, Christopher Robin politely patronizing, but from the Introduction to *Winnie-the-Pooh* to the last words of the last sentence of *The House At Pooh Corner,* Pooh is the center of our author's attention, and therefore of ours. Right away let us remember that ancient Hindus named the seven stars of the Great Bear after the Seven Rishis, or Seers, and their function was to transmit the wisdom of the past to us in the present. Precisely what our Great Bear does.

The overriding importance of Pooh means that we must examine the relevant astrological data to the fullest extent that our present state of knowledge makes possible.

Let us begin by applying the same method that proved so illuminating when applied to some of his friends. That is, let us try to deduce Pooh's sun sign from his behavior. We shall find the results deeply significant.

The first story in *Winnie-the-Pooh* tells us that he "lived in a Forest all by himself." Ah, we might think to ourselves, a loner. The text might seem to confirm this when it goes on to say that Winnie-the-Pooh lives "under the name of Sanders." Not only a loner, but one so shy that he conceals his real name. Rashly we might then jump to the conclusion that he is a Virgo. As we go on, however, we find he is noticeably gregarious. Milne tells us of a typical Pooh day plan.

One day when Pooh was thinking, he thought he would go and see Eeyore, because he hadn't seen him since yesterday . . . he suddenly remembered that he

*hadn't seen Owl since the day before yesterday . . . he
began to wonder how Kanga and Roo and Tigger were
getting on . . . And he thought, "I haven't seen Roo for a
long time, and if I don't see him today it will be a still
longer time."*

All this walking and talking with his friends, visiting their houses, receiving them in his own, might
suggest Gemini (May 21–June 21) or perhaps Sagittarius—with the Sagittarian tactlessness corrected, perhaps by an ascendant Libra (September 23—October
23). We might well find confirmation of this when we
begin the list of titles attributed to him toward the end
of Chapter Nine: "F.O.P. (Friend of Piglet's), R.C. (Rabbit's Companion)." But how does it go on? "E.C. and
T.F. (Eeyore's Comforter and Tail-finder)."

This honorific reminds us that his decision to find
Eeyore's tail brought a rare and remarkable tribute
from Eeyore himself.

*"Thank you, Pooh," answered Eeyore. "You're a
real friend," said he. "Not like Some," he said.*

And this was no isolated incident. The very page
on which these titles of Pooh are listed occurs as we are
reading of his courageous and ingenious rescue of the
floodbound Piglet. A less dramatic but more lasting ex-

ample of his generosity was his invitation to the eventually homeless Piglet to share Pooh's home. These repeated examples of friendliness—we have mentioned
only a few of the most striking—might easily lead us to
label him an Aquarius (January 20–February 18).

But then let us examine an important and much
misunderstood part of his lifestyle: his diet. Incredible
as it is to any serious reader of the Pooh cycle, there
are, I fear, some who still labor under the absurd delusion that Winnie-the-Pooh is greedy! They base this
ridiculous notion on the text's frequent references to his
eating or thinking about food. Even on the most literal
interpretation, this shows grossly careless reading. Have
such readers never noticed that it is nearly always

"a *little* something" (my emphasis) or the semantically equivalent "smackerel" that Pooh is talking about?

These repetitions stress Milne's picture of Pooh as a studiously moderate eater. Readers who add obstinacy to superficiality may defend their position by pointing to the incident when Pooh gets stuck in Rabbit's doorway. " 'It all comes,' said Rabbit sternly, 'of eating too much.' " And Pooh, having become "a Wedged Bear in Great Tightness" has to fast for a week.

The correct interpretation is obvious to all who have considered the characteristics of the sun sign Libra, the Balance. The balance of a Libran is by no means a dull level or a rigid fixity. On the contrary, it is maintained by frequent adjustments. An unvarying adherence to any one course would be essentially *un*-balanced. Pooh maintains his perfect equilibrium by balancing his normal moderation by occasional feasting and occasional fasting.

Should any further evidence of this interpretation be needed, we find it stated in the plainest language in our text, which always supplies the true answer to the honest searcher. "I don't get any fatter." These are the words of the foremost authority on the matter: Pooh Bear himself. This should settle the question once and for all. Just in case, however, some doubts linger, let us look where our author has placed this clinching statement. It is in Chapter Four of *The House At Pooh Corner,* well on in the Ursinian saga. If Pooh had regularly overindulged in food, it would certainly have shown by this time. As it is, we now know that his well-planned, additive-free diet, plus his regular Stoutness Exercises and frequent walks have kept his body as well as his mind in perfect Libran balance.

Further research would demonstrate that it would be equally tempting to assign Pooh Bear to all the rest of the zodiacal signs. The more perceptive readers have doubtless already grasped the significance of this. They will understand that no single sun sign can do justice to the infinite variety of the Enormous Brain of Pooh. It contains them all. Meanwhile, let us look at the astrological implications of some other Milnean messages, or "missages," as he has taught us to call them.

Even before we read the title page of *Winnie-the-Pooh,* we examine, or should examine, the map of the World of Pooh. Its importance is signalled by its position in the volumes: at the beginning and at the end. The Alpha and Omega of this Book of Revelations. As if this were not enough, Milne tells us that this map was "DRAWN BY ME [CHRISTOPHER ROBIN] AND MR SHEPARD HELPD." Thus doubly authenticated, this map, as we should expect, contains level upon level of mystical meanings. For the moment, let us look only at the first direct reference to Pooh himself. At the extreme left, there is a portrait of him sitting on a log in front of his door, and the legend reads "POOH BEARS HOUSE."

Looking at the rest of the map, we find KANGAS HOUSE, RABBITS HOUSE, MY HOUSE, OWLS HOUSE and PIGLETS HOUSE. In our pilgrimage along the Ursinian path, we shall enter all these houses, and have their inner arcana revealed, not only in Milne's words but also in Shepard's drawings. And we have already mentioned that beautiful passage where Piglet nobly sacrifices his own house to Owl and is invited to share Pooh's.

Thus houses are mentioned again and again in the World of Pooh. Now "house" has an important technical meaning in astrology. Just as the sun completes its circle of the zodiac in a year, our earth completes the same circle in twenty-four hours. Hence we have another division of the zodiac into twelve. Astrologers call these divisions "houses." While the sun signs indicate our general abilities, the houses point to the way we use those abilities, each in our own lives.

Our house is calculated from the position of the Ascendant—the sign of the zodiac that is rising on the eastern horizon at our birth—and the Midheaven—the highest point the sun reaches on that day. As with Pooh's sun signs, the infinite variety of his nature makes it impossible to place him under the domination of any one Ascendant. How then are we to explain this impossibility? The text, as always, gives us a clue. On the second page of the Introduction, we read that cryptic reference to Pooh in the Polar Bears' house. Apart from the obvious allusion to the great constellation of the Polar sky, we must interpret the abhorrent absurdity of Pooh Bear imprisoned in a cage as a warning that it would be equally absurd to limit him in any way, even by the limits of the greatest constellation.

Following this clue, we remember the variety of names by which the great northern constellation is known. And we note the obvious parallel with Winnie-the-Pooh, who is also known by so many names: by abbreviations such as Winnie, Pooh, Bear, variations such as Pooh Bear, alternatives such as Edward Bear; moreover, he lives "under the name of Sanders." True names, as ancient tradition has always taught, require deep knowledge of what is named. The many names of the Great Bear, both as character and constellation, confess our human inability to discover any one name that would encapsulate the essence of either of these two mighty powers.

Astrologically, as in all other sciences, esoteric as well as exoteric, the Great Bear transcends all analysis. May I remind readers of the Sanskrit original that lies behind *arktos,* the Greek name for the constellation? The Sanskrit name is *rakh,* which means "to be bright." Pure brightness is what enables us to examine other things, but in itself it dazzles all examination. We shall understand more of this when we come to the Qabalah. Later too we shall say more about the Polar mysteries. Yet even here we can see how all this applies to Winnie-the-Pooh.

A Warning from Pooh Bear

Like all the occult subjects, astrology has its dangers as well as its rewards. As we should expect, the wise and benevolent Bear gives more than one warning to those who ponder his words with the proper care. I have already mentioned the significance of the bee episode. Remember also Pooh's Heffalump Trap. The Heffalump, Pooh predicted, would fall into the Very Deep Pit, because he was looking up at the sky, wondering if it would rain or if it would stop raining: in either case, trying to read the future from the sky. This, I am happy to say, is in perfect accord with many of the best modern astrologers, who stress the dangers of prediction, and urge us to learn self-knowledge rather than prophecy from the stars.

In the days when astrology was most revered, one of its principal applications was finding the most propitious moment for making and executing important plans. Physicians, for example, consulted the stars for diagnosis; sometimes telling their patients that their illness was caused by an evil starry influence, hence our "influenza" or "flu" today. Similarly, successful treatment had to wait for the right astrological moment. This, no doubt, explains Pooh's emphasis on time when reflecting on his therapeutic restoration of Eeyore's tail:

> *Who found the Tail?*
> *"I," said Pooh,*
> *"At a quarter to two*
> *(Only it was quarter to eleven really),*
> *I found the Tail!"*

Starry influences were equally important in alchemy, to which we now turn.

3

POOH AND THE
ALCHEMISTS

At the beginning of A. A. Milne's very first Winnie-the-Pooh story, Christopher Robin asks him to explain what he meant by saying that Winnie-the-Pooh lived "under the name of Sanders." "It means he had the name over the door in gold letters." Many readers must have been surprised to find gold letters over Pooh Bear's door. These letters suggest a rather ostentatious opulence, out of keeping with his usual simple comfort. Can we believe that for once he was guilty of an error of taste?

This absurd hypothesis we can dismiss at once. We have already established that if ever Pooh appears at fault, the fault is always in ourselves and never in him. Our more alert readers have doubtless already understood the mention of gold as a reference to alchemy; for the best-known purpose of alchemists was to transmute base metals, such as lead, into gold. As alchemy is the subject of this chapter, readers may occasionally find a certain obscurity in it. This is perfectly in accord with alchemical tradition. For example, the second-century alchemist Cleopatra—several important early alchemists were women—began her discourse by saying, "Now I will tell you clearly . . . and I will begin by speaking in riddles."

The riddles were as often pictorial as verbal. So it is natural that Shepard's illustrations make a vital contribution to our chapter on alchemy. We have already looked at the picture of Winnie-the-Pooh sitting on a stone in the middle of a river and sunning himself. Then we examined its astrological meaning, and we noted that astrology was intimately connected with alchemy. Now we shall examine the strictly alchemical significance of this picture.

First of all, we read "The sun was so delightfully warm." Now the sun, or Sol, was central to alchemic thought; it was specially linked with gold. Even today, the sign for gold is the same as the sign for the sun. Moreover, metaphor and allegory were the normal language of alchemists. So we can be sure that Pooh's happy relationship with the sun means allegorically that his alchemical work had attained success, that he had achieved transmutation into gold.

This is only a beginning. The stone Pooh is sitting on is in the middle of a stream. Now water was no less important than the sun. In alchemical language, it was often equated with Luna, the moon. Just as on the material plane, both sun and water are essential to life on earth, so alchemically too their union was essential. Illustrations in sixteenth- and seventeenth-century alchemical works often depict the union of Sol and Luna or the union of different chemicals with the image of a wedding or even copulation. And the offspring of this alchemical wedding was the Philosopher's Stone, the essential element in all transmutations.

There is more to come in our study of this picture. We established in the previous chapter that the insect flying in the center background is clearly a dragonfly. The dragon or serpent played an important role in alchemy. It represented the material that alchemists began with and which they had to destroy as the first stage of transmuting it into something more precious. This destruction they often referred to as slaying the dragon.

Contemplating the first stage of the Great Work inevitably makes us think of the last: the production of the Philosopher's Stone. And of course it is there staring us in the face: the warm stone Pooh is sitting on. The very fact that he is sitting on it is significant too. It indicates his assured control of it. No wonder he "had almost decided to go on being Pooh in the middle of the stream for the rest of the morning."

So here, beyond a shadow of doubt, we have a

great allegorical design, showing the prime agents of the Work: Sol and Luna (in its guise of water), the Dragon as the first stage, the Stone as the successful conclusion, and Pooh Bear in calm control, at ease with the world and his own spirit, having triumphed in both kinds of alchemy, as we explain below.

The Two Kinds of Alchemy

Alchemy was of two kinds: physical and spiritual. Physical alchemists aimed either at transmuting base metals, such as iron or lead, into gold, or at finding the Elixir of Life, which could cure all diseases and prolong life, perhaps indefinitely. Just as physical alchemists tried to raise the lower to the high kind of metal, so the spiritual alchemists aimed at raising themselves to the highest possible spiritual plane. In practice, many alchemists worked both spiritually and materially.

We have just seen Pooh's double triumph allegorized in Shepard's picture. As always in the Pooh opus, we shall find ample confirmation that we are following the correct—that is the Ursinian—train of thought. While we are still in the first chapter of *Winnie-the-Pooh,* we find the episode of Pooh, the tree, the bees and the balloon—another example of the multiple meanings to be found in every episode of our texts.

The Alchemical Significance of the Bees

All readers will remember that Pooh was walking in the Forest when he heard a buzzing-noise. He thinks: (1) "If there's a buzzing-noise, somebody's making a buzzing-noise"; (2) "The only reason for making a buzzing-noise that *I* know of is because you're a bee"; (3) "The only reason for being a bee that I know of is making honey"; (4) "And the only reason for making honey is so as *I* can eat it."

Having concluded, by this rigorous logical process, that the buzzing of bees entails the presence of honey for him to eat, Pooh climbs the tree in search of it. A branch gives way under him and down he falls.

Undaunted, he borrows a blue balloon from Christopher Robin, rolls in black mud, and then, "Pooh Bear floated gracefully up into the sky." The bees become suspicious and one stings Pooh. He decides, "These are the wrong sort of bees." And he concludes, ". . . they would make the wrong sort of honey." And he returns to earth.

Even this bald outline tells us a good deal about the alchemical meaning of this incident. Pooh's search for honey obviously symbolizes the alchemist's search both for gold—the honey-colored metal—and for the honey of truth and spiritual achievement. Still more obviously than the tree, the balloon symbolizes the ascent to the higher regions of knowledge and virtue, free from all earthbound trammels.

Let us, however, examine this profound and multi-layered passage in more detail. It will amply repay the effort. As Pooh climbs, "he sang a little song to himself":

> *Isn't it funny*
> *How a bear likes honey?*
> *Buzz! Buzz! Buzz!*
> *I wonder why he does?*

Leaving our readers to explore the meaning of this Hum beyond the obvious connection of the mystical bear with truth and wisdom, we pass on to the Complaining Song that follows. Complaining is so unusual in Pooh that it clearly signals something special:

It's a very funny thought that, if Bears were Bees,
They'd build their nests at the bottom *of trees.*
And that being so (if the Bees were Bears),
We shouldn't have to climb up all these stairs.

Guided by our now well-established knowledge
that honey here symbolizes alchemic wisdom, we see
that Pooh is telling us that this wisdom cannot be attained by the earthbound but calls for a strenuous ascent to higher planes.

Pooh's fall from the tree puts this interpretation
beyond all reasonable doubt. However high the tree
may be, it is essentially rooted in the earth. The breaking of the branch demonstrates that we cannot rely on
any such ladder to rise to the heights of alchemical wisdom. I hope it is unnecessary to remind my readers that
Pooh, of course, knew this perfectly well. He was simply providing us with an object lesson. If any doubts
linger in your mind, just look at the calm manner in
which he analyzes the situation as he falls. Note that he
"spun round three times"—a mystical number—before
he "flew gracefully into a gorse-bush."

In the light of what we now know, the reason for
his change of method, from tree to balloon, is plain
enough. The change from earthbound tree to free-
floating balloon needs no explanation. Neither should I
need to repeat that the balloon is symbolic were it not

that Christopher Robin took it literally. But Christopher Robin, though a pleasant boy, was noticeably earth-bound. He repeatedly shows himself deaf to the inner meanings of Pooh. In the vivid phrase of the Apoc-ryphal Epistle to Barnabas, he heard the words of the master but he heard them with uncircumcised ears.

Having got the balloon, "Winnie-the-Pooh went to a very muddy place that he knew of, and rolled and rolled until he was black all over." I daresay that many of my readers—very understandably—are less familiar with alchemy than with *Winnie-the-Pooh*. Therefore they may fail to notice that when Pooh rolled in the mud, he was reminding us of the very foundation of al-chemical theory.

We all know that physical alchemy aimed at trans-muting base metal to gold. Alchemists were confident this was possible because they believed that all actually existing materials were simply different forms of an un-derlying, original Prime Matter. A belief, incidentally, more consonant with modern than with nineteenth-century physics. Now, in the terms of the sort of book Milne was writing, what could be a better symbol of Prime Matter than black mud? Our confidence in this interpretation is confirmed when we remember that the great seventeenth-century alchemical scholar, Dr. Robert Fludd, represented Prime Matter as black and formless. It is also significant that Pooh knew this muddy place. Nowhere else does he show any interest in mud, so obviously this passage is a coded message telling us that Pooh was familiar with the alchemical theory of Prime Matter.

We now come to one of those passages which have often been shockingly misunderstood. I refer to the confrontation with the bees, particularly with the bee that stings him.

Heat and Alchemy

I suppose many of us have experienced a bee sting. What was our first sensation? A burning sensation. Precisely: burning, a sensation of heat. In the context of our present studies, this inevitably reminds us that heat was of the greatest importance in alchemy. The stages by which some base metal was to be transmuted to gold were accomplished by varying degrees of heat. Heat was vital both to the theory and the practice of alchemy. Theoretically, alchemists believed they were merely assisting and hastening the work of nature. Nature, they held, always aimed at perfection. Lead was, so to speak, on its way to becoming gold. Natural gold was the final result. Heat, the external heat of the sun producing the internal heat of the earth, was the vital agent of this process. And the alchemists had to discover and apply the appropriate kinds of heat to speed up this process.

So much for the theory. In practice, controlling their fires to give and maintain the proper heat at every stage was as difficult as it was important. Thomas Norton, the fifteenth-century alchemist, was typical when he wrote:

> *A parfet Master ye maie him call trowe [true],*
> *Which knoweth his Heates high and lowe*
> *Nothing maie let [hinder] more your desires*
> *Than ignorance of Heates of your Fiers.*

Armed with this knowledge, we have no difficulty in interpreting Pooh's next comment after he has been stung: "I have come to a very important decision. These are the wrong sort of bees." Therefore, he judged, "They would make the wrong sort of honey." He means, of course, that the heat was wrong—as he had just experienced. Inevitably, therefore, this attempted transmutation would fail to produce true gold, the right kind of honey.

We can now understand the episode of Christopher Robin's bath, at the end of Chapter One. This has long puzzled Ursinian scholars. Christopher Robin was obviously a well-brought-up boy, and one would take it for granted that a pre-bed bath was part of his normal routine. But it seems hardly relevant to the main interests of our studies.

Now, though, with our minds attuned to alchemy, we remember that a bath was one of the principal vessels used in the Work. It was also one in which reaching and maintaining the right temperature was vital: a task which demanded constant vigilance. Christopher Robin himself clearly knew this. It explains his otherwise curious question: "Coming to see me have my bath?" In view of the importance of unremitting vigilance, how are we to explain the staggeringly casual reply: " 'I might,' I said"? Actual carelessness is, of course, out of the question. An obvious explanation leaps to mind: "I"—presumably A. A. Milne himself—knows by now that Christopher Robin, amiable boy though he is, was as yet unready for intellectual or spiritual transmutation. He should be comfortable and safe in his bath, but anxious precision concerning the temperature would be a waste of time.

This explanation is corroborated when we look, as we always should, at the relevant illustration by E. H. Shepard. This shows Pooh Bear sitting on the end of the bath, by the taps. Perhaps he was checking the heat? Careful examination undermines this interpretation. No part of him is touching the water, nor is he holding or looking at any kind of recording instrument.

Moreover, if we look at his eyes and facial expression, they show relaxed ease or possibly rapt contemplation of some mystical vision, but not concentrated attention on Christopher Robin or the temperature of his bath. Pooh also knew that Christopher Robin, though admirably fitted for the ordinary pursuits of his class and period, was not the stuff of a Magus.

However this may be, inability to reach or maintain the correct heat was one of the three common causes of alchemical failure—the other two being impure ingredients and fragile vessels. Having warned us of the difficulties and dangers of alchemy, Pooh goes on to show something of its rewards.

Physical Transmutation

All Ursinologists who have read John Donne's "Love's Alchymie" will remember the words

> *And as no chymique yet th'Elixar got,*
> *But glorifies his pregnant pot,*
> *If by the way to him befall*
> *Some odoriferous thing, or medicinall.*

And they will have recognized immediately the reference to the pot of honey that plays so large a part in the World of Pooh.

At first, Donne's verse seems to undermine the alchemist's claims. Donne denies that any "chymique" (alchemist) ever achieved the Elixir, and says alchemists boasted of *any* accidental discovery, sweet-smelling or medicinal, they chanced on during their experiments. Donne, of course, knew enough about alchemy to be aware that it worked on more than one level, each with its own value. On the most material level, Donne may have been thinking of the discovery in 1510 of Benedictine, the oldest known liqueur, by the Benedictine monk and alchemist, Dom Bernardo Vincelli. Vincelli might well have glorified the pregnant pot that gave us that delicious golden liquid.

Just as Vincelli doubtless enjoyed Benedictine,

Pooh Bear certainly enjoyed honey on a purely material level. He was no sour ascetic, but a true follower of the Golden Mean. (Note the implications of that traditional phrase.) But there was far more to it than that. I hope no one will doubt that honey also represents gold, and so Pooh's honey pot represents sometimes the still of a successful alchemist, sometimes the container in which the transmuted material was later stored. Even successful transmutation has its dangers. When Pooh suggests baiting the Heffalump Trap with honey, he is warning us that greed for gold may trap us in a pitfall. Later, we find Pooh himself is at the bottom of the Heffalump Trap and cannot see his way out because his head is jammed in the honey pot: a dramatic parable of blindness caused by immersion in material possessions.

All too many readers have seen this as evidence of Pooh's greed and comic absurdity. From our perspective, of course, we realize that Pooh was demonstrating the dangers of successful transmutation. Can we doubt for a moment he was thinking of alchemists who were murdered for their secrets, or imprisoned by powerful men as a source of gold? The strangest of these stories concerns Johann Friedrich Bottger (1682–1719), who spent several years as a prisoner of the Elector of Saxony. Bottger failed to produce the gold demanded by his master, but he did succeed in discovering a method of making porcelain. As the discoverer of Dresden china, he ended his short life restored to the Elector's favor. But he was exceptionally lucky.

Pooh's rigorously scientific approach appears in the way he examines the pot of honey before he takes it to the Heffalump Trap. The pot is in his larder, and is labelled "HUNNY." Living in a world of allegory and metaphor, an alchemist would be the last person to take a literal meaning for granted. A glance assures him that it looks like honey. Looks, though, can be as misleading as words. " 'But you never can tell,' said Pooh. 'I remember my uncle saying once that he had seen cheese just this colour.' "

Pooh was well aware that attempts at transmutation often produced something that looked like gold but did not stand up to analysis. Sometimes this was the result of fraud. Sometimes of genuine error. We must remember that much that passed for ordinary gold was impure. Some alchemists too maintained that *their* gold was superior to the natural product. Pooh, as we should expect, scorned both dishonesty and dubious argument. He tested for indubitable gold, and tested thoroughly until he could say, "I *was* right. It *is* honey [i.e., gold], right the way down."

Different Levels of Alchemy

All the authorities agree that a successful alchemist needed the highest moral and spiritual qualities as well as knowledge and skill. These were essential for success even in psychical alchemy; much more, of course, for those whose aims were spiritual. Our general knowledge of Winnie-the-Pooh should be enough to convince us that in these respects he was qualified in the highest degree. In any case, we have already seen that Shepard's allegorical masterpiece shows that Pooh had succeeded in the Great Work (or Grand Magisterium of Alchemy, as it was often called), which he could not have done if he had been deficient morally or spiritually.

We next meet honey when Winnie-the-Pooh is taking a pot as a birthday present for Eeyore, who is even more depressed than usual because no one has remembered his birthday. We note in passing that Pooh's benevolent plan for comforting Eeyore is characteristic of the high moral standards traditionally required of alchemists. All readers of Pooh will remember that he ate the honey on the way, and eventually presented Eeyore with an empty jar, suitably described, as "a Useful Pot to Keep Things In."

All those who have read this book so far will confidently reject the ridiculous notion that Pooh showed greed in eating the honey and hypocrisy in pretending the empty pot was an acceptable present. But they may be sure his actions were justified without quite understanding what the justification was. I am happy to enlighten them.

First, on the material plane, honey would not have been a particularly suitable gift for Eeyore, who preferred thistles. Equally, material gold would have been useless to him in the uncommercial World of Pooh. The spiritual gold of the higher alchemy would have been quite out of Eeyore's reach. Pooh's profound knowledge of his friend therefore checked his first generous impulse, and he gave Eeyore a present perfectly suited to his personal capacity for happiness and understanding.

We are not told whether Eeyore ever tried alchemy himself, but if he did, we may be sure that his limitations showed, naturally enough, in his alchemical potential. We know that his favorite food was the thistle. In alchemical terms, this clearly symbolizes the use of vegetables in the Work. The great Chinese alchemist Ko Hung said that these were adequate only for minor projects, such as producing hairy feet, long ears and sexual potency. Our text and its illustrations make the long ears and hairy feet plain enough. Writing in the 1920s, Milne could not mention sexual potency in a work ostensibly addressed to children, but in a franker generation, the Reverend Sydney Smith (1771–1845) praised an article in the *Edinburgh Review* as "long but vigorous like the penis of a jackass." The fit is perfect.

I must now deal with another objection I have heard raised against Pooh's conduct in this episode. Some sour critics, who have passed the age of innocent enjoyment without reaching the age of mature wisdom, brutal realists of twelve or disillusioned cynics of thirteen, ask, What was the point of giving Eeyore a pot to put things in? What sort of things? they ask. What sort of things can we imagine Eeyore possessing that he would want to keep in a pot?

It is characteristic of all great teachers to stimulate their pupils rather than to spoonfeed them. Pooh knew that once Eeyore owned the pot, it would stimulate his mind to think of something to put in it. As we know, the "something" suggested itself at once, in the shape of Piglet's burst balloon. Can we doubt that Pooh foresaw that sooner or later Eeyore would move beyond his immediate pleasure in putting the balloon into the pot and taking it out again? That then the burst balloon would make him think of an inflated balloon? And that finally this symbol of rising above the earth would fire Eeyore with the ambition to ascend to a higher mental plane than that symbolized by the "thistly corner in the forest" where he lived?

Pooh and Piglet: The Alchemist as Rescuer

The next Ursinian incident involving the mystical pot occurs in Chapter Nine of *Winnie-the-Pooh*, which describes the Terrible Flood—and this will be dealt with fully in Chapter Eight. Pooh was dreaming he was at the East Pole, getting colder and colder. He woke up to find his feet in the water, and water all around him.

So he took his largest pot of honey and escaped with it to a broad branch of his tree, well above the water, and then he climbed down again and escaped with another pot . . . and when the whole Escape was finished, there was Pooh sitting on his branch, dangling his legs, and there, beside him, were ten pots of honey. . . .

The number of pots is gradually reduced until, "Four days later, there was Pooh . . ."

It was on this day that he received the famous "missage" from Piglet. Piglet had been marooned in his tree-dwelling and had written an appeal for help, put it in a bottle and thrown it on to the water, which carried it to Pooh.

No reader of that chapter can have forgotten the superb combination of generosity, courage and practical ingenuity with which Pooh organized and carried out the rescue of Piglet. He used an empty honey jar to float to Christopher Robin. He then converted Christopher Robin's umbrella into a boat, which brought them to Piglet.

Even Christopher Robin was startled out of his usual blindness to his friend's wisdom. "Christopher

Robin could only look at him with mouth open and eyes staring, wondering if this was really the Bear of Very Little Brain whom he had known and loved so long."

We are all familiar with this passage. But are we all equally familiar with the esoteric connection between the revelation of Pooh's intellectual and moral greatness and the disappearance of the ten pots of honey? I fear not. Never mind: Enlightenment is at hand.

On the material plane, the honey in the pots sustained Pooh corporeally and strengthened him for the physical ordeal. Spiritually, it prepared him for this supreme example of wisdom and loving kindness. As always, the text gives a vital clue to those who read it with the devoted attention it demands.

What was the vessel which carried Pooh to Christopher Robin? *The Floating Bear,* one of the empty honey pots; that is, the alchemical vessel, physically empty, having served its turn, but spiritually full, full of the air which is the breath of inspiration—which literally means breathing in—the divine afflatus, the *prana* of Hindu mysticism. What more compelling evidence can there be that Pooh was as triumphant in spiritual as in physical alchemy?

If even Christopher Robin can, just for a moment, be struck with wonder at this revelation of Pooh's greatness, can we be less?

Pooh as an Example of the Benevolent Alchemist

Pooh's general benevolence appears not only in his friendly warmth to all his companions but in signal acts of practical help. The rescue of Piglet was one example out of many. It was Pooh who undertook the task of searching for and finding Eeyore's missing tail. We note that finding lost objects was a common attribute of occult adepts.

We are happy to note also that Christopher Robin completed the good work by nailing the tail back in its proper place. So often have I had to call attention to his limitations that it is particularly pleasant to celebrate his practical kindness. I repeat that his good nature is undoubted; so is his practical competence for everyday tasks: It is his intellectual powers that fall so far short of our hero's.

Another example of Pooh's practical benevolence is his readiness to help in the search for Small—Very Small Beetle, to give him his full name. Who can remember this and not also remember Ko Hung on the qualifications of an alchemist? He must "love even the creeping things," as with Small; "rejoice in the good fortune of others," such as sharing his game of Poohsticks with his friends; "commiserate with their sufferings," as he did with Eeyore many times, with Owl when his house was destroyed, and with Piglet, when he was marooned and when he lost his home. We notice that the Search Organdized for Small is immediately preceded by Pooh's counting his pots of honey. The totals were fourteen or fifteen. Let me point out that the number of his pots of honey—symbolic gold—is a vivid concrete realization of the alchemical process of multiplication; the process by which the Philosopher's Stone produced gold in quantities enormously greater than the Stone itself.

Pooh as a Great Alchemist on Every Level

The juxtaposition of success in physical alchemy with success in spiritual alchemy is one of the most striking proofs of Pooh's status as a supreme master of his craft. We add that his fame is now approaching that life of a hundred years which Dr. Johnson considered the mark of literary immortality: clear evidence that Pooh had also attained the Elixir of Life. So I think you will agree that Winnie-the-Pooh is one of those rare exceptions mentioned by Ko Hung some sixteen centuries ago: "Those wishing to enter the path are as numerous as the hairs of a buffalo, while the successful are as rare as the horn of a unicorn."

Pooh himself warns us of the elusive nature of the quarry in similar terms: The improbable Heffalump and mysterious and undiscovered Woozle are *his* metaphors for the difficulties of the search.

4

POOH AND THE
HERMETIC PHILOSOPHY

The Hermetic philosophy or Hermetism is named after its supposed founder, Hermes Trismegistus. In many areas it overlapped other kinds of Ancient Wisdom. Hermetists studied astrology, alchemy and the Qabalah. But they had two special characteristics: 1. They claimed they had developed a technique for rising, step by step, from the earthly plane to the highest spheres of mind and spirit. 2. They also claimed they could use the powers of the heavenly bodies to influence events in this world.

Before we let Pooh explain further, we must first observe some of his relevant symbolic acts. Unless we do so, we may deviate from the straight and narrow path of firm evidence into those vacuous regions where chimeras bombinate. This danger is ever present to those who explore the mysterious regions of the occult.

So now let us observe a familiar scene: the first and last paragraphs of *Winnie-the-Pooh*:

1. *Here is Edward Bear, coming downstairs now, bump, bump, bump, on the back of his head, behind Christopher Robin. It is, as far as he knows, the only way of coming downstairs, but sometimes he feels that there really is another way, if only he could stop bumping for a moment and think of it. . . . Anyhow, here he is at the bottom, and ready to be introduced to you. Winnie-the-Pooh.*

2. *. . . I heard Winnie-the-Pooh*—bump, bump, bump—*going up the stairs behind him [Christopher Robin].*

There are the first and last paragraphs. Note that each is accompanied by a Shepard drawing. Of course, we know already that Shepard's illustrations play a vital part in the Pooh opus. Nowhere, though, is this more striking than when we deal with Hermetic lore. Paintings, diagrams and statues were as important as the written word in conveying the Ancient Wisdom of the Hermetic Magi. Indeed, in some respects, they were more important. In the first place, visual symbols could be more effective than words in conveying occult meanings to the initiate while veiling them from the profane outsider. Additionally, such images had a magical power

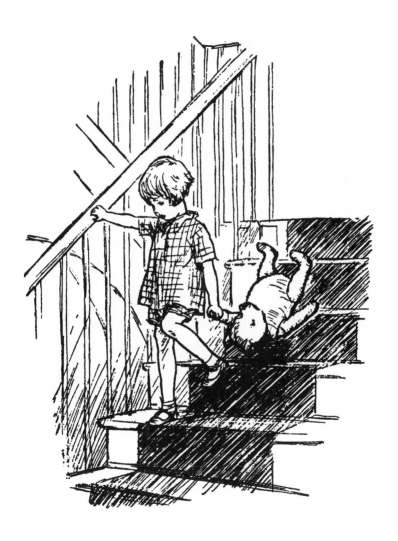

when operated by a skilled Magus. Now let us return to Pooh's staircase.

Even without the privileged enlightenment of Hermetic lore, we immediately notice two arresting facts. First and most obviously, we begin with a descent and end with an ascent. Second, less strikingly but equally important, our sage is first referred to as "Edward Bear." It is only when he has reached the bottom that he is introduced as "Winnie-the-Pooh."

Take the second and simpler problem first. We can see at once that the rather bewildered bear, who makes an uncomfortable and undignified descent of the stairs, is a mere mask or persona of the Great Bear whose wisdom we are humbly studying. Milne makes it all clear to us by using the label "Edward Bear" for the mere mask, and waiting till the descent of the stairs is complete before introducing us to "Winnie-the-Pooh."

We should give full weight to the word "introduce." It is derived from a Latin word meaning "to lead inwards." It has been said that a word never entirely forgets its origin. We may be confident, therefore, that when Milne *introduced* us to Winnie-the-Pooh, he was leading us into the mystery of the Great Bear. Only a little way, of course. We have seen that no one name could exhaust that great essence. And the alert reader will remember the deeper revelation hinted at by the form "Winnie-the-Pooh"; a revelation that Milne, in

true Hermetic fashion, explicitly refuses to elucidate.

But surely, you will be thinking, there is more to it than this? Something more specifically Hermetic? You are quite right, there is more. The Hermetists' aim was to rise from the lowly sphere of earth to the utmost pinnacles of spiritual and mental power. This could not be achieved at one bound. It was a long and arduous ascent of the cosmic ladder or—in Milne's own image—*stairway*.

The Hermetists envisaged the universe as a vast series of concentric circles. At the center, which, it is essential to remember, was also the bottom of the universe, was the earth. Then came the circles of the other three elements: water, air and fire. Then the circles of the planets, which for them included the sun and the moon. Then the circle of the fixed stars. This was the outer limit of the material world, but beyond that came the realms of pure intellect, culminating in supreme and ultimate Mind (*Mens* or *Nous* in Hermetic terminology), dwelling in the Empyrean. The ascent to Mens or Mind was therefore easily pictured as the ascent of a staircase or ladder.

We now have no difficulty in interpreting the allegory of the stairs in our two paragraphs. The descent at the beginning means that Pooh as Hermetic Magus is kindly descending to spread virtue and wisdom in our lower world. The puzzled and somewhat unkindly treated Edward Bear symbolizes our initial failure to recognize his true nature.

Pooh Bear's control of an apparently more perilous descent is strikingly displayed in his fall from the tree in a later chapter. This is in marked contrast to Tigger's difficulty in descending his tree when it is shown that "Tiggers Don't Climb Trees": a warning of the dangers of attempting to scale the mystical heights without due preparation.

When we look at the last paragraph of the last chapter, we find no reference to Edward Bear, no signs of any puzzlement; simply the information that Winnie-the-Pooh is going upstairs. This indicates in the plainest possible manner that Winnie-the-Pooh, having diffused light and wisdom on earth, is now returning to the loftiest intellectual and spiritual plane.

Ursinologists who are also familiar with *The Divine Comedy* will naturally be reminded of Beatrice's leading Dante up through the heavenly spheres till they reach the supreme heights of the Empyrean. Yet another of the significant parallels between Dante and A. A. Milne. In case any readers missed this particular esoteric significance, in the stairs (and the tree), they are reminded in that multivalent image of the balloon, which so clearly freed Pooh to "soar upwards through the cloudy veil" (Giordano Bruno, quoted on page 236 of Frances Yates's *Giordano Bruno and the Hermetic Tradition*). In this little allegory, Pooh's own cooperation in his descent exemplifies his willingness to help his weaker friends on the Way.

That is why Shepard's picture of the stairs conveys a message of hope to all of us. We notice that Kanga, Eeyore and Piglet are on the landing. After we have investigated Chapter Ten, we shall not be surprised to find Kanga here. Piglet's presence may surprise us at first. On reflection though, we can understand that it is prophetic of his development in *The House At Pooh Corner.* It is the presence of Eeyore and Christopher Robin that demands explanation, and this will be given in Chapters Seven and Eight.

Pooh and Giordano Bruno

Though Winnie-the-Pooh is incomparably the greatest bear in history, he is not the only important bear, or even the first. Early in the twelfth century, we find Bruin the Bear in the popular collection of fables, *Reynard the Fox.* So popular was this character that "Bruin" became a synonym for "bear." Bruin: Every student of the Ancient Mysteries must immediately think of Bruno, Giordano Bruno (1548?–1600), the famous Hermetic philosopher of the Renaissance, and every Hermetic Ursinologist, putting together the two names—Bruno and Bruin—must immediately think of Winnie-the-Pooh.

It is just possible that some readers may consider the connection somewhat tenuous, may even dismiss it as a mere verbal coincidence. To this I would reply, first, that in the area we are now exploring, there are no *mere* coincidences. All coincidences, verbal and otherwise, are profoundly significant. Second, the verbal connection will be corroborated by overwhelming evidence. Pooh Bear himself will reveal the essentials of the Hermetic philosophy in the course of this chapter. For the moment, it is enough to say that Hermetism was ranked so high in the Renaissance that when its texts arrived in Florence in about 1460, Cosimo de' Medici commanded his great scholar Marsilio Ficino to set aside his translation of Plato and concentrate on translating the *Corpus Hermeticum.*

In the Renaissance, people revered the Hermetic writings largely because they believed that their author was the legendary Hermes Trismegistus—Milton's "Thrice-Great Hermes." They identified him with the Egyptian god Thoth and the Greek Hermes, and dated him at the very latest as contemporary with Moses. So the Hermetic texts had the double prestige of possibly divine origin and certainly vast antiquity. This prestige was undermined in 1614, when Isaac Casaubon proved conclusively that the Hermetic documents had in fact been composed by various writers between the first and third centuries A.D. Indeed, some of the texts proved to be of even more recent date. Naturally, many Hermetists strongly resisted this painfully disillusioning discovery. We must at least wonder if Milne was hinting at this when he says that "Christopher Robin had spent the morning indoors going to Africa and back." As Egypt was the home of Thoth and the traditional source of the Hermetic documents, Christopher Robin's indoor journey to and from Africa tells us that he had spent his morning studying the *Corpus Hermeticum*. If so, his Hermetic studies redound to his credit but perhaps the passage also suggests he still accepted their traditional origin. Christopher Robin's somewhat conservative attitude would make him a suitable representative of those who held by traditional beliefs and rejected disturbing new discoveries.

Despite a strong rearguard action, Casaubon's dating eventually had to be accepted. However, the true value of the Ancient Mysteries and the Ancient Wisdom does not depend ultimately on dates. There is a truth of events, and this we must strictly respect; but there is also a truth of ideas and imagination. This too deserves our respect. All will be well as long as we do not confuse the two. This little book takes the greatest care to avoid any such confusion. For example, having faithfully recorded the facts about the dates of the Hermetic writings, we now continue, just as faithfully, to record the facts about the basic Hermetic ideas. First we must keep our promise to demonstrate convincing evidence of a connection between Giordano Bruno and Winnie-the-Pooh. Once again we turn to that deeply enigmatic Introduction to *Winnie-the-Pooh*. We can explain the puzzling and painful references to Pooh's being behind locked doors and shut in a cage—however special—in one obviously relevant way. They clearly refer to Bruno's emphatic assertion that unless Hermetic wisdom is revealed, "a great prince in prison lies . . . suffocating in the close air of a narrow prison house." Happily, Pooh Bear does not lie for long in his prison. The whole World of Pooh is precisely the revelation that Bruno demanded.

The World of Pooh that Milne reveals to us is a world where Pooh walks in light and freedom, not one where we can approach him only "through dark passages." He mingles freely with his friends, spreading happiness to all and healing to the afflicted. Why then did our author, who wrote nothing without good cause, begin with this passage, so dark in meaning, symbolically as well as literally? The answer is precisely Hermetic, and Hermetic on several levels.

1. It alludes to the dictum which Bruno puts into the mouth of Isis: "Fate has ordained a vicissitude of darkness and light." Obviously, no material cage could imprison the spirit of Winnie-the-Pooh. No darkness could obscure the radiance of his mind. The darkness must lie in the minds of unenlightened outsiders.

2. It is *their*—perhaps, we must admit even *our*—minds that are imprisoned in ignorance. Here we may call for support on Shakespeare. We pointed out in Chapter One that he was a great Magus, and we shall demonstrate it later in this very chapter. For the moment, though, just let us remember that he made Feste declare, "I say there is no darkness but ignorance" (*Twelfth Night*, IV.2.43).

3. Like Milne, Bruno has his own difficult passages. Many Ursinologists must have been shocked and puzzled to read his invocation to the gods to "remove from the heaven of our minds the BEAR of deformity." Bruno doubtless lessened their shock but hardly their puzzlement when he soon added, "To Ursa Major and Ursa Minor there ascend Truth, Being, Goodness, which drive out Deformity, Falsehood and Defect." Happily, Pooh Bear himself solves the puzzle.

As before, the solution lies partly in learning to separate Pooh as he truly is from Pooh as our limited minds perceive him. Text and illustration repeatedly emphasize Pooh's close relationship with the sun, reminding us that solar magic is a key concept in Hermetism, as in much Neoplatonic thought. Summing up the arguments of the last few paragraphs, we now understand the difference between the Bear of Deformity as he might appear to our unaided senses, and the radiant Bear which our author and his illustrator privilege us to see. If any lingering doubts remain, Milne's own emphatic statement must dispel them. Describing Pooh sunning himself, he tells us, "Pooh had almost decided to go on being Pooh in the middle of the stream for the rest of the morning . . ." Could he have given us a more convincing statement of the Great Bear's serene contentment with his true self?

How the Hermetic Magus Manipulates the Heavenly Bodies

This naturally leads us to another important strand in Hermetic philosophy. The chapter on astrology dealt with the more conventional aspects of the subject: the heavenly bodies' connection with and possible influence on earthly beings and events. Hermetic philosophers went a step further. They believed that a true Magus could *use* the stars. He could canalize the influences that poured down from the stars and planets to everything on earth. Robert Fludd, the English Hermetist and Qabalist (1574–1637), said, "There is not any plant or herb which hath not a star in the firmament." And he added, "Moses Arabicus saith that every animated thing hath a peculiar star, which sendeth down his influence to defend and preserve his life upon earth."

Everything in the universe—and Bruno, remember, believed in an infinity of worlds—everything was connected with everything else. Each planet had a particular influence over certain plants, animals and minerals. Each sign of the zodiac was specially related to particular parts of the body. A Magus who knew these relationships could use them to enlist these vast cosmic powers to assist his own labors. Thus, in addition to natural relationships, a skilled Magus could construct talismans and images that would draw down planetary influences and enable him to manipulate them.

This explains a passage in *The House At Pooh Corner* which has often proved a stumbling-block to Pooh's admirers. One sunny morning, Pooh finds Piglet planting an acorn, in the hope that it will grow into an oak-tree and provide him with a convenient source of acorns.

"Well," said Pooh, "if I plant a honeycomb outside

my house, then it will grow up into a beehive." This has often been taken—by the superficial—as an amusing absurdity of the Bear of Little Brain. The wiser have often found it an insoluble problem. Thinking Hermetically, the answer is plain. Hermetic thinking is fundamentally analogical, so why should a honeycomb not grow into a beehive, just as an acorn grows into an oak? Of course, this does not happen without special help, and it is precisely this sort of help that a Magus can provide by manipulating the heavenly powers.

Even in this brief example then, Pooh was demonstrating both the great Hermetic maxim, "As above, so it is below," and his own power as a Magus. Typically, he also warns us of the dangers of using powers we cannot control. If, he reminds us, "the wrong piece" of a beehive were used by mistake, the result might be bees that were "buzzing and not hunnying." It is another example of our author's skill that he places this little incident early in the chapter entitled "In Which It Is Shown That Tiggers Don't Climb Trees." Here, Tigger, overconfident in his powers, carries Roo up a tree but cannot get down without help. Whether we take the incident literally or symbolically, the warning is equally valid.

No wonder that every Magus emphasized the need for strict secrecy to prevent powerful knowledge falling into incapable or perhaps unworthy hands. This, no doubt, is why Milne veiled such mighty truths under the form of a children's tale.

Even today, when the time has come to reveal much of the Ursinian wisdom, I continue to respect the principled secrecy of my illustrious forerunners. Readers will search these pages for information that would

give them power far beyond the reach of nuclear fission.

It is no mere chance that Hermetism has bequeathed to ordinary usage the term "hermetically." When we say that a vessel is hermetically sealed, we mean that it is sealed in the closest possible way, so that nothing can leak from it. Literally, Hermetic sealing was essential for the vessels used in alchemy, a science practiced by many Hermetic philosophers. Metaphorically, secrets unsuited to the ignorant and unworthy were hermetically sealed in the minds of the adepts. There were, of course, times when actual vessels had to be opened and secrets had to be revealed. We see a dramatic example of this when the Wedged Bear in Great Tightness is released from Rabbit's door "just as if a cork were coming out of a bottle." This simile leaves us in no doubt about the Hermetic reference. On the spiritual and intellectual level, it means that the time had come for Pooh, after his retreat for fasting and meditation on the Sustaining Book, to return to our world and give it the benefit of his wisdom.

This kindly and unselfish giving of his wisdom is but one of the ways in which Winnie-the-Pooh fulfills Bruno's criteria of the true Hermetic Magus. He is "temperate"—remember "a *little* something" (my emphasis); "expert in the arts of healing"—remember how he restores Eeyore's amputated tail; "remarkable in divination"—remember his discovery of the North Pole;

and the way home when Rabbit had lost all his friends in the Forest mist. The overwhelming evidence of his enduring popularity confirms Bruno's prediction concerning the Hermetic Magi, that "the vestiges of their amazing prowess endure unto this day."

Pooh and Shakespeare

The powers of a true magus were well summarized by Shakespeare's Prospero in a famous speech near the end of *The Tempest*. Addressing the spirits he controls, he says:

> *. . . by whose aid,—*
> *Weak masters though ye be,—I have bedimm'd*
> *The noontide sun, call'd forth the mutinous winds,*
> *And 'twixt the green sea and the azured vault*
> *Set roaring war: to the dread rattling thunder*

Have I given fire, and rifted Jove's stout oak
With his own bolt: the strong-based promontory
Have I made shake: and by the spurs pluck'd up
The pine and cedar: graves, at my command,
Have waked their sleepers, op'd, and let them forth
By my so potent art.
(V.1.40–50)

This passage alone demonstrates Shakespeare's deep and accurate knowledge of Hermetic magic. The powers attributed to the witch Sycorax (V.1.269–270) show he knew all about black magic as well as white. Can we doubt that Winnie-the-Pooh's powers were greater than Prospero's, and exercised more gently and benevolently? Compare, for example, Prospero's first meeting with Ferdinand to Pooh's first meeting with Tigger.

Prospero greets the noble and courteous Ferdinand with churlish suspicion, calls him a traitor and impostor, and uses his magical arts to enslave him (I.2). How very different is Pooh's treatment of Tigger!

"Winnie-the-Pooh woke up suddenly in the middle of the night and listened." He hears a continued noise: "*Worraworraworraworraworra,*" which he realizes is unfamiliar.

"What can it be?" he thought. "There are lots of noises in the Forest, but this is a different one. It isn't a

growl, and it isn't a purr, and it isn't a bark, and it isn't the noise-you-make-before-beginning-a-piece-of-poetry, but it's a noise of some kind, made by a strange animal."

In this situation, where many would have evinced fear, Pooh shows the calm courage of the truly enlightened Magus. Where Prospero would have reacted with hostile suspicion, and defended himself by magically paralyzing Tigger, Pooh greets him courteously, invites him in for the night and promises him breakfast. If any have ever doubted Pooh's spiritual and moral superiority, surely this episode must convince them. Prospero himself implicitly acknowledges his own inferiority when he promises to abjure his *"rough"* magic" (my emphasis). How different from the more gentle but—per-

haps because—more potent magic of Winnie-the-Pooh.

We note also that this incident shows Pooh exercising a proper caution when he introduces himself:

> *"I'm Pooh," said Pooh.*
> *"I'm Tigger," said Tigger.*

Hospitable though he is, Pooh gives only part of his name. For he understands that knowing a complete name gives the knower power over the known; a power it would be foolish to confide to a stranger. The impulsive, and probably uninstructed, Tigger unhesitatingly volunteers his whole name.

When Pooh gives Tigger the promised breakfast, he is not only practicing hospitality, he is also testing Tigger's suitability for occult initiation. Alas! Tigger rejects the proffered honey of wisdom. The end of the chapter, however, gives Pooh grounds for qualified hope. Having also rejected Piglet's haycorns and Eeyore's thistles, Tigger settles enthusiastically for Roo's Extract of Malt. Both in taste and texture, this is far nearer to honey, to which, perhaps, he will one day graduate. We notice that the use of food to indicate the eater's intellectual state follows the example of that famous occultist, Abbot Trithemius (1462–1516), who warned against revealing truths to the unsuited in the phrase "Hay to an ox and sugar to a parrot. . . ."

The Hermetic Meaning of Pooh's Hums

"Poetry and Hums aren't things which you get, they're things which get *you.*"

Thinking Hermetically, we cannot fail to recognize the connection between the Hums of Pooh and the Orphic Hymns. Renaissance Hermetists attributed these hymns to Orpheus, the mythical ancient Greek musician whose music was so powerful that it enchanted wild beasts, trees and rivers. Orpheus was regarded as one of the masters of Ancient Wisdom, immediately following Hermes Trismegistus himself, and followed by Pythagoras and Plato.

The earliest Orphic Hymns were probably composed about the sixth century B.C., but the collection best known in the Renaissance probably belongs to the second or third century A.D. the same period as the Hermetic writings. Many of these later Orphic hymns were invocations to the sun, and we have a clear parallel in Winnie-the-Pooh's poem:

> *This warm and sunny Spot*
> *Belongs to Pooh.*
> *And here he wonders what*
> *He's going to do.*

The first two lines establish the typical Orphic connection between the sun and the Magus. The third and fourth show "the warm and sunny spot" as particularly suited to meditation and decision on future action. At this point though, I feel bound to anticipate a possible objection. Critics whose knowledge of the Milnean text is greater than their understanding of it may point to the next two lines and try to use them to challenge the whole concept of Pooh which this work is dedicated to establishing. The lines they refer to run as follows:

> *Oh, bother, I forgot—*
> *It's Piglet's too.*

These lines, they argue, show Pooh revelling selfishly in the exclusive enjoyment of a private and solitary paradise. Worse than that, he expresses regret and anger when he remembers he has to share that paradise with Piglet. The intensity of his anger, they add, is proved by his use of the word "bother," the strongest expletive Milne permitted himself to use in a work ostensibly written for children. These lines, they say, are not only decisive in themselves, but they also cast a dark backward shadow on such incidents as Pooh's consumption of the honey originally destined for Eeyore's birthday present.

These arguments might appeal to the less balanced apostles of deconstruction. These, and other exponents of modern theory, might even accuse me of a naively simplistic interpretation of the texts we are examining. Far from this, I reply, my whole commentary is based on the concept of multiple levels of meaning, of multivalence (plurality of values) and polysemy (multitude of meanings). How else could two comparatively short works contain coded references to astrology, alchemy, Hermetic philosophy, Druidism, the tarot, the Female Mysteries, in a mere two hundred pages?

However, though the Ursinian texts can—indeed, should—be interpreted in many ways, there are limits. No less eminent a semiotician than Professor Umberto Eco has stated that however many legitimate interpretations of a text there may be, some interpretations are self-evidently illegitimate. I hope that by now all my readers will unhesitatingly agree that any interpretation hostile to Winnie-the-Pooh is self-evidently illegitimate.

I hope they will be equally ready to agree that the only acceptable interpretation of Pooh's "bother" is that it expressed regret that he had for a moment forgotten his little friend. Seen in this light, "bother" is not a euphemism for some more violent expletive, but the strongest term that his serene nature would ever need.

Summary of Winnie-ther-Pooh as Hermetic Magus

I think Winnie-ther-Pooh—only his full title suffices here—has now demonstrated his credentials as a Hermetic Magus.

1. The Hermetic ascent from earth to the highest reaches of intellect is presented three times, in the three allegories of ascent: by the staircase, by the tree and by the balloon. Three is always a mystical number, but it carries particular significance when linked with Thrice-Great Hermes.
2. Shepard's allegorical picture of Pooh sunning himself on the stone in the river depicts the solar relationship the Hermetists emphasized so strongly. Pooh spells this out in:
3. His Orphic Hymn.
4. Together, these solar references strongly suggest that he could not merely interpret the heavenly bodies, as we saw in Chapter Two on astrology, but could also use and in a manner control them—as his thoughts on planting part of a honeycomb so strongly suggest.
5. His vast powers went hand in hand with a temperate life and the warm practical benevolence we see on countless occasions, a conformity specially stressed by Giordano Bruno.

Looking at the whole World of Pooh in the light of Hermetic tradition, we inevitably see it as a restatement, in its own terms, of the mystical city of Adocentyn, supposed to have been founded by Hermes Trismegistus himself. In this city, "the inhabitants were made virtuous and withdrawn from all wickedness and harm." Adocentyn is perhaps the archetype underlying many later Utopias. All of these, like it, have a certain coldness. Despite their virtues, should we really enjoy living in any of them? Only in the Pooh cycle do we find a Utopia where peace and virtue join with warm, varied and convincing enjoyment.

5

POOH AND THE
TAROT

Though many of my readers are doubtless familiar with the tarot cards, others will probably appreciate a brief account of them.

A tarot pack consists of seventy-eight cards. These are divided into two main groups: the Greater Arcana or Major Trumps, of twenty-two cards; and the Lesser Arcana or Small Cards, of fifty-six cards. The small cards are divided into four suits: Batons, also called Wands or Clubs; Cups; Swords; Coins or Pentacles. Each suit consists of numbers one to ten, plus four court cards: King, Queen, Knight and Knave or Princess.

Some occultists claim great antiquity and equally ancient esoteric (secret) meanings for this pack. In fact, it seems to have come into existence during the fifteenth century, and was used just for such exoteric (publicly known) purposes as card-playing and fortune-telling. During the occult revival of the nineteenth century, traditional packs were interpreted esoterically, and new esoteric variants were produced. Several of these were based on a close connection of the tarot with the Qabalah. The two following quotations show how widely opinions of the tarot can vary.

"The Tarot was the sole book of the ancient Magi," wrote that eminent occultist Eliphas Levi (*ca* 1810–1875), who called it "this key of all doctrines and all philosophies of the old world." Levi was a stimulating but often wildly unreliable writer. We should balance his opinion against the comment of the great Qabalistic scholar Gershom Scholem, who roundly condemned "the activities of French and English occultists . . . [for] their own totally unrelated inventions, such as the alleged kabbalistic origins of the Tarot-cards."

Fortunately, we have already taken account of the vital distinction between the study of facts and the study of ideas. So we can accept Scholem's judgment that the tarot did not originate from the Qabalah, while maintaining that the Qabalah is a valuable tool in elucidating the esoteric meaning of the Milnean texts, especially in relation to the tarot.

In this chapter, I take an eclectic view of the tarot, referring to six of the best-known packs, both esoteric and exoteric. As I go, I identify the packs I am using, so that readers with their own packs should be able to compare their interpretations with mine.

Eeyore and the Tarot

Though every chapter of the Milnean opus contains level upon level of esoteric lore, some chapters are outstandingly rich, even among their companions. One of these is Chapter Four of *Winnie-the-Pooh*, where we first meet Eeyore and read his first recorded conversation with Pooh. We find Eeyore in the Forest, thinking about things. "Sometimes he thought sadly to himself, 'Why?' and sometimes he thought, 'Wherefore?' and sometimes he thought, 'Inasmuch as which?'—and sometimes he didn't quite know what he *was* thinking about." While Eeyore is in this puzzled state, Pooh arrives.

> *"And how are you?" said Winnie-the-Pooh.*
> *Eeyore shook his head from side to side.*
> *"Not very how," he said. "I don't seem to have felt at all how for a long time."*
> *"Dear, dear," said Pooh, "I'm sorry about that. Let's have a look at you."*

As soon as Pooh has a look at Eeyore, he realizes the trouble.

"Why, what's happened to your tail?" he said in surprise.

"What has *happened to it?"* said Eeyore.

"It isn't there!"

Having confirmed the loss by his own inspection, " 'That Accounts for a Good Deal,' said Eeyore gloomily. 'It Explains Everything. No Wonder.' "

Looking at the problem tarotically, if I may coin the word, Pooh understands it immediately. At once, he remembers the Fool in the exoteric tarot packs (Wirth, Marseilles and Authentic English). These show a dog tearing at the Fool's breeches and baring his bottom. The parallel with the tailless Eeyore is emphasized in Shepard's illustrations.

The wise and benevolent Bear moves swiftly from intellectual understanding to practical solution. " 'Eeyore,' he said solemnly, 'I, Winnie-the-Pooh, will find your tail for you.' "

Let us dwell for a moment on the exact manner and wording of his promise—remembering that every Milnean word combines the most delicate precision with unplumbed depths of meaning. Note that Pooh speaks solemnly; and solemnity is rare with him. Announcing his name at length adds weight to his promise. In a word, Pooh himself underwrites Eeyore's own judgment that the loss of his tail "Accounts for a Good Deal"—even that "It Explains Everything."

When Pooh has recovered the lost tail and, with Christopher Robin's help, restored it to its proper place, "Eeyore frisked about the forest, waving his tail so happily . . ."

How does this link with the tarot? The answer is plain as soon as we look at one of the most popular esoteric packs, the Waite-Rider pack. Here the Fool is a handsome young man, fully and elegantly clothed. His dog bounds at his heels in a friendly way. Other esoteric packs have important differences but they all show the Fool as a figure deserving respect.

We can now interpret Eeyore's transition from gloom to joy as a step from the earthly plane, symbolized by the exoteric cards, to the higher planes, symbolized by the esoteric. Naturally, it was Winnie-the-Pooh who recognized that Eeyore was ready for another step in his mystical progress. Acting as a true guru, he gave him the necessary help. His action here has a double significance. It throws light both on Pooh and on Eeyore.

In spite of the Fool's improved appearance in the esoteric cards, I suspect that Eeyore's many admirers will protest at my identification of this much loved character with the Fool. Let them be patient. They will soon see that identifying Eeyore with the Fool in the tarot is far from insulting him. On the contrary, it gives him a much more important position than even his warmest admirers have ever conceived. Let us just look at the multiple significances of the tarot Fool. The number of the Fool, you will remember, is zero. In the Ancient Mysteries, zero stood for the elemental chaos of nothingness out of which the universe was formed. This formation naturally needed the assistance of some mighty plastic power. In this case, the power was, of course, Winnie-the-Pooh, whom we have just seen in action.

This reminds us that the bear used to be regarded as especially symbolic of this shaping process. It was long believed that the bear cub was born shapeless and was literally licked into shape by its mother. On the mental and spiritual plane, this is precisely what Pooh Bear continually does. Further evidence that Pooh cannot be confined to a single gender role.

Though Eeyore's mind is somewhat confused when we first meet him, Pooh must already have brought it out of primeval chaos. Eeyore may not be able to answer his own questions, but the very fact that he asks them shows an awakening curiosity about the great mysteries of life. This is perfectly in keeping with the traditional character of the tarot Fool. He is essentially a questor; young, inexperienced and ignorant, but vigorous, and eager for knowledge and experience.

In light of what we now know about Eeyore, his first recorded meeting with Pooh demands examination in depth. We have established that Pooh has brought Eeyore out of total chaos. From their brief conversation, we can confidently infer that Pooh is now visiting his charge to see how he is progressing. His "How are you?" is not the conventional polite formula of greeting: It is more like a physician's enquiry of a patient. Similarly, Eeyore's answer—"Not very how"—does not misuse or misunderstand the word "how," as superficial readers have supposed. It expresses a quite understandable uncertainty about his mode of existence—the how of his existence—in his rapidly evolving world.

Crowley's Thoth pack is particularly informative about the Fool. He speaks of the Great Fool of Celtic tradition, and links him with Perceval, whom we shall discuss in Chapter Seven. His powerful Green Man is a traditional symbol of spring and reawakening life, and so of fertility.

Crowley gives us another visual identification of the Fool with Eeyore. Instead of the dog that assails the Fool in the medieval packs, or bounds after him in the Waite version, Crowley's Green Fool has a tiger attached to his thigh. I say "attached" as it is not clear whether the tiger is biting or nuzzling the man. This ambiguity clearly refers to the incident of Tigger, Eeyore and the river in *The House At Pooh Corner.*

Pooh, Piglet, Rabbit and Roo were playing Poohsticks when they saw Eeyore floating in the river. Once Eeyore was ashore, Rabbit and Roo asked how he had come to be in the river.

"Somebody BOUNCED me. I was just thinking by the side of the river—thinking, if any of you know what that means—when I received a loud BOUNCE."

Tigger arrives and is accused of bouncing Eeyore into the water. After some prevarication, he admits, "Well, I sort of boffed."

Though Eeyore was indignant at first, soon after, "Tigger and Eeyore went off together, because Eeyore wanted to tell Tigger How to Win at Poohsticks." Like Tigger, Crowley's tiger skillfully suggests both the aggressive and the friendly interpretations. It thus places the identification beyond all doubt.

Kanga: A Character with Multiple References to the Tarot

In the last chapter, we saw the gentle power with which Winnie-the-Pooh controlled the "bouncy" and potentially dangerous Tigger. Next morning, they sat down to

breakfast, only to discover that Tigger, though profess-
ing to like everything, does not like honey. They soon
discover that he does not like Piglet's haycorns or
Eeyore's thistles either. So they go to see if Kanga can
give Tigger breakfast. "They told Kanga what they
wanted, and Kanga said very kindly, 'Well, look in my
cupboard, Tigger dear, and see what you'd like.' Because she knew at once that, however big Tigger
seemed to be, he wanted as much kindness as Roo."
Her benevolent control here unmistakably indicates another tarot identification.

We are left in no doubt that Kanga's treatment of
Tigger was highly successful. We can be sure that it was
not only his taste for Extract of Malt that kept him a
permanent and welcome resident in Kanga's house. She
trusted him to go off with her beloved Roo "to have a
nice long morning in the Forest." And this when she
"felt rather motherly."

Kanga's relaxed control of Tigger is duplicated in
the tarot Queen of Wands, who has an attendant leop-
ard in the Thoth and Golden Dawn packs. Female control over one of the big cats is portrayed in all the Major
Trumps labelled "Strength," and in Crowley's equivalent, characteristically labelled "Lust." They show a
woman dominating a lion or, in the Crowley pack, the
seven-headed Beast of the Apocalypse.

All of these obviously symbolize Kanga's handling

of Tigger, but there are important variations. The Golden Dawn comes closest to the text, as it shows a woman in effortless control of her lion. The Marseilles woman impressively but rather brutally forces the lion's jaws open. Waite's woman is similar but slightly less violent. Crowley's naked woman is riding her strange mount with apparent ease, though perilously poised.

At this point, some readers may complain that I am being unduly eclectic; that moving as I do from one pack to another may suit my convenience but is painfully lacking in intellectual rigor. My answer is that, as we agreed in Chapter Two that no one sun sign was adequate to the limitless genius of Winnie-the-Pooh, so his World inevitably transcends the limits of any one tarot pack. It is, I maintain, entirely legitimate to use clues wherever we find them; always provided, of course, that they are in no way distorted to fit a preconceived interpretation.

This also answers those who dismiss Crowley's interpretations as excessively personal. It is inconceivable that mere accident produced so many connections between the Thoth pack and the World of Pooh. What was the source of these connections? Now Crowley had reached his essential conclusions about the tarot in 1912, fourteen years before Milne published *Winnie-the-Pooh.* How did he gain such intimate knowledge of the great texts? His own explanation would probably have been that all this, like so much else, was revealed to him by his Secret Masters. To an occultist, what explanation could have seemed more natural? Of course, his commentary, *The Book of Thoth*, did not appear until 1944, so he may well have supplemented his earlier ideas by studying Milne's published works. There is no doubt, moreover, that Frieda Harris, who created the images for the Thoth pack, played a more creative role than her official description, "Artist Executant," suggests. Crowley himself said she "possessed in her own right the Essential Spirit of the Book."

The chapter "In Which Kanga and Baby Roo Come to the Forest" contains Piglet's statement that "a Kanga was Generally Regarded as One of the Fiercer Animals." This combination of female gender with formidable power and maternity clearly refers to another of the Major Trumps: the Empress. She is always enthroned, holding the regalia of imperial rule, and often visibly pregnant. This combination of immense power with fertility is clearly symbolic of Kanga in terms of the tarot. Her pouch is as near to a pregnant womb as Milne could get in a book for children in the 1920s.

Kanga's confidence in her own power appears strikingly when Roo is kidnapped. Piglet warns his friends, ". . . it is well known that, if One of the Fiercer Animals is Deprived of Its Young, it becomes as fierce as Two of the Fiercer Animals." Yet when Kanga real-

izes what has happened, she does not display ferocity because she knows after a moment's thought that no harm will come to Roo. "So she said to herself, 'If they are having a joke with me, I will have a joke with them.'" And she proceeds to put Piglet through Roo's bedtime routine, bathing him—to his great discomfort and indignation—and giving him Roo's medicine, so that he won't "grow up small and weak like Piglet." Her joke shows the relaxed confidence of an Empress assured of her position and of the respect due to it.

The final paragraph of this chapter tells us that "every Tuesday Kanga spent the day with her great friend Pooh, teaching him to jump." The full significance of this will appear only in Chapter Ten, but meanwhile we can observe this special friendship as confirming the symbolic relationship of Kanga with the tarot Empress.

Piglet

Piglet's role in the Kanga–Roo episode was not altogether impressive, but its place in his progress, including the very first mention of him in the Introduction, will be analyzed in Chapter Eight. The important fact now is to concentrate on his final promotion to the status of Pooh's resident disciple. This is the climax of a gradual process.

Early on, we see him as one of the crowd pulling Winnie-the-Pooh out of Rabbit's doorway. This establishes him from the beginning as a helper of Pooh. The relationship is confirmed on his second appearance, when Pooh honors him by inviting his company on a quest of the Woozles; a quest not without peril, as Pooh says: "Would you mind coming with me, Piglet, in case they turn out to be Hostile Animals?" Throughout the two volumes, we always find Piglet loyal and affectionate, if sometimes uncomprehending.

In terms of the tarot, his final acceptance as Pooh's *chela* would ally him either with the Page, as pupil and follower, or with the Prince, as a destined successor. It is hard to accept that Pooh would ever have or need a successor, so let us examine the tarot Page.

At once we meet a problem. The exoteric packs do show a Page or the equivalent Knave, but the esoteric packs, except for Waite's, show instead Princesses. The easy solution would be to ignore the esoteric packs and concentrate on the exoteric. But by now, I hope my readers have learned to mistrust easy solutions. Taking the easy path would mean omitting essential Qabalistic connections. It was doubtless because Waite considered these too arcane for public knowledge that he suppressed what he certainly knew. However, these Qabalistic connections are essential to understanding Piglet's symbolic importance.

Explaining the cards still leaves a problem about Piglet. Can we really take him as the representative of a tarot Princess? I hope to demonstrate that we can. That in fact he represents the Princess of Cups. We have already seen enough examples of cross-gender identifications to know that Piglet's maleness in no way debars him from representing a Princess.

The Princesses of the esoteric packs share one vital factor with the Pages or Knaves of the exoteric packs: All are essentially helpers. For example, the commentary on the Golden Dawn pack, while emphasizing the formidable power of a Princess, adds, "Yet her power existeth not save by reason of the others." Crowley says, "People described by this card are very dependent on others, but at the same time helpful to them." Could we have a better description of Piglet? Before his final allegiance to Pooh, he showed a comparably dependent attitude to Christopher Robin.

This, of course, is not all. The Princess of Cups represents the earthy part of the element of Water. This puzzling concept is effectively dramatized in Chapter Nine of *Winnie-the-Pooh*, "In Which Piglet Is Entirely Surrounded by Water."

At first Piglet finds the Flood exciting rather than alarming. His only regret is that he has no one to share his excitement with. This typical dependence on others is stressed by his listing the ways in which the others would deal with the Flood. His own anxiety grows as the earthy element in him feels overwhelmed by the rising waters. Yet he forms and executes a successful plan—sending a "Help" message in a bottle—though, typically, one that depends on others for its success.

All readers will now accept the identification of Piglet with the Princess of Cups; if any doubt remains, our author has taken pains to dispel it when he tells us in the Introduction that Christopher Robin "once had a swan (or the swan had Christopher Robin, I don't know which) and that he used to call this swan Pooh." Now the swan is symbolic of the Princess of Cups, who wears a cloak of swanlike feathers in the Golden Dawn pack. Note also that the transfer of the name "Pooh" from swan/Piglet to Winnie-ther-Pooh manifests the special relationship which we now know is a main theme of the Pooh cycle.

Rabbit

I hope that by now, my readers have gained sufficient confidence to trust interpretations that may not seem obvious at first sight—always provided, of course, that closer examination will reveal convincing support. Bearing this in mind, let us look at six different packs depicting "The Universe" or "The World" (one of the Major Trumps). All show a minimally draped woman surrounded by a round or oval border. Outside this border, in the corners, we see, reading clockwise from the top left, the heads of a man, an eagle, a lion and an ox. What does this remind us of in the World of Pooh?

Which of Pooh's friends has the most numerous and most varied friends-and-relations? Rabbit. As for number, Rabbit himself says that, if, like Kanga, he carried his family about in his pockets, he would need eighteen: one for his handkerchief and seventeen for his family. As for variety, his friends-and-relations include mice, beetles, a hedgehog, a weasel or perhaps a stoat, and a number of unidentified insects. "Rabbit had so many friends-and-relations, and of such different sorts and sizes, that he [Pooh] didn't know whether he ought to be looking for Small at the top of an oak-tree or in the petal of a buttercup."

This was when Rabbit had "organdized" a search

for the missing Small. This "organdizing" or "Captain-ish" activity was typical of Rabbit. In a key passage, we read that "Rabbit brained out a statement." Now, as far as my researches have gone, this use of the verb "to brain" is unique to this passage. Its nearest and perhaps only precedent is in Shakespeare's *Cymbeline,* and even there it means to understand rather than to create in the mind. Milne must have had a very powerful reason for such a strange use of the word. Clearly he wanted to call very special attention to it. He wanted us to register Rabbit's purely intellectual approach. And not merely intellectual, but intellectual in a markedly material and physiological manner. The context adds that Rabbit applies his somewhat earthbound intellect to organizing others. In a word, to administration. Now, the tarot Universe card is Qabalistically connected with the thirty-second Sephirotic Path, which the Golden Dawn commentary labels precisely "the Administrative Intelligence." So here we have irrefutable evidence from an independent source to confirm the already compelling internal evidence that connects Rabbit with the tarot Universe card.

Pooh

But what, you must be asking, about Pooh himself? Obviously, we could fill volumes with relevant and illuminating thoughts about Pooh and the tarot. So here, most of all, we must select.

Already we have several times probed the mystical meanings of the scene where Pooh sits on a stone in the river, basking in the sun. Its meanings are far from being exhausted. In the tarot, the sun is described as the "Collecting Intelligence." The signs of the zodiac are powerful in themselves, but they emanate from the sun, which is central to them and their influences. Just as, Milne repeatedly makes clear, Pooh Bear is central to all the creatures in the Forest. By a paradox which is typical of occult wisdom, the Bear of Little Brain is in fact the Collecting Intelligence of all the Forest inhabitants. He confides this secret to us in his Anxious Pooh Song, when he confesses, "Well, Pooh was a Bear of Enormous Brain."

On two occasions in *Winnie-the-Pooh,* our hero's preeminence is so spectacular that even his most im-

mature companions and most superficial readers are
bound to recognize it. I refer, of course, to his discovery
of the North Pole (Chapter Eight) and his rescue of
Piglet (Chapter Nine).

Near the end of the Quest for the Pole, Shepard
shows Pooh holding a pole across the river for the
"swimming" Roo to catch hold of. A few pages later,
we see the same pole, now discovered to be the
North Pole, stuck in the ground, with the appropriate
notice:

NorTH PoLE
DICSovERED By
PooH
PooH FouND IT

The shape of the pole is markedly similar to the staff on the Ace of Wands in the Waite pack, and not very different from that in the Marseilles pack. Then we remember that the Aces are traditionally placed in the North Pole of the Universe, a universe they govern with unseen, often unrecognized but irresistible power, just as Pooh governs his World, and this, of course, further identifies him with the constellation Ursa Major.

When we come to Pooh's second most obvious triumph, the rescue of Piglet from the flood, the problem, as it is so often with Pooh, is not to find a significant mystical connection, but to choose from the throng of candidates. It is always wise to be guided by the words and pictures that together compose the subject of our study. Two themes predominate in the relevant chapter (Nine). These are water and pots.

The first picture we see in this chapter is Piglet looking out from his beech-tree house, which is completely surrounded by water. Two pages later, we see Pooh sitting on the branch "of his tree," with ten pots of honey beside him. The text, as always, is in that symbiotic relationship with the pictures, which is typical of the Pooh revelation.

Approaching this incident tarotically, what parallel springs irresistibly to mind? Obviously that with the Major Trump called "The Star." All versions of this card show water and all show pots, except Crowley's, which shows goblets. The identification could hardly be indicated more strongly. As we shall see later, the Qabalah describes the Path associated with this card as the path of Natural Intelligence: the Natural Intelligence that Pooh demonstrated in his ingenious use of an empty honey pot to float him to Christopher Robin, and then of Christoper Robin's inverted umbrella to sail them both to Piglet. Pooh's links with both the Ace of Wands and the Star are merely two of the many possible identifications and show once again that he cannot be narrowly circumscribed.

As we leave the tarot, we notice the frequency of tree imagery in this chapter. We have commented on Piglet's tree house and Pooh's branch. Christopher Robin's house too is in a tree. Studying the Ancient Mysteries as we are, this emphasis inevitably compels us to think of the archetypal Ancient Men of the Trees: the Druids, to whom we now turn.

6

P O O H   A N D   T H E
D R U I D S

A Caution

Druids existed over two thousand years ago, and organizations of Druids exist among us today. The relationship between ancient and modern Druids is a matter of some controversy. Happily, these controversies need not concern us as Ursinologists. The Great Bear transcends all such problems. His serenely eclectic approach shows, I think we may confidently assume, that he was fully aware of the problems. It is all the more remarkable that he showed this awareness in the 1920s, before the researches so admirably summarized by the recent work of Ronald Hutton. Further convincing proof of the deep wisdom of Winnie-the-Pooh.

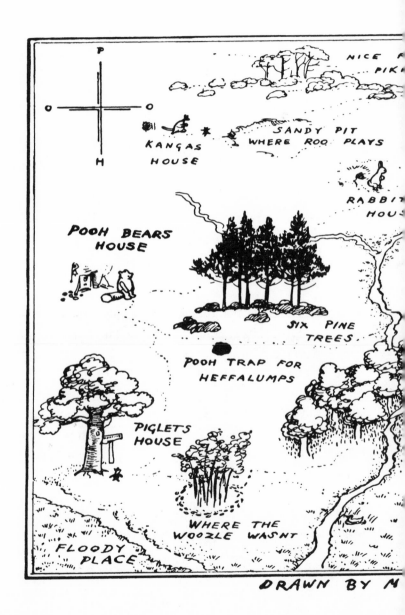

DRAWN BY M

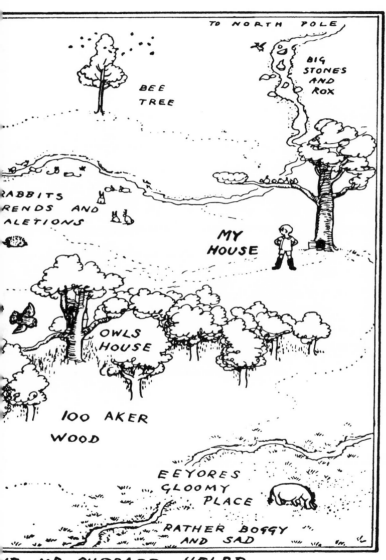

TO NORTH POLE

BEE TREE

BIG STONES AND ROX

RABBITS RENDS AND ALETIONS

MY HOUSE

OWLS HOUSE

100 AKER WOOD

EEYORES GLOOMY PLACE

RATHER BOGGY AND SAD

D MR SHEPARD HELPD

Significance of the Endpapers

All serious Ursinologists begin their studies with the Alpha and Omega of Milne's *magnum opus.* That is, they begin with the illustrated map at the beginning and end of the mystic text. The placing of this map and its doubling emphasize its importance, and this is further stressed by the words at the bottom: "DRAWN BY ME AND MR SHEPARD HELPD." Nowhere else is the joint authority of writer and artist so explicitly invoked. Why? we are bound to ask. Surely Milne and Shepard must have wanted to draw our attention to something of great significance which they feared might be overlooked.

Let us therefore look again and most carefully at the map. And let us not be afraid to state the obvious. Again and again we have found that the obvious has been glanced at but not properly seen. The most striking impression we get from the map is the amazing preponderance of trees. The clump—larches, we discover later—WHERE THE WOOZLE WASNT; PIGLETS HOUSE—a tree; the SIX PINE TREES; the BEE TREE; MY HOUSE—a tree; OWLS HOUSE—a tree; and 100 AKER WOOD.

Even by the standards of blindness we have gotten used to, it is staggering that no one has previously noted the glaring fact that in our present context the World of Pooh is a world of Druids.

Exactly what sort of men and women the ancient Druids were and what they did are matters of controversy, but no one doubts their essential connection with trees. Though the *Oxford English Dictionary* derives the name "Druid" from a Celtic word for a magician, many Druidic scholars derive it from a word meaning wood-sage or oak-seer. As we are here concerned with the Ancient Mysteries, not with ancient history, we can ignore dates and origins and concentrate on what Druidic beliefs contribute to the Mysteries. Above all, we must look at what Winnie-the-Pooh has to tell us about them.

Pooh and the Trees

Studying the Milne–Shepard map, we notice that, unlike Piglet, Owl and Christopher Robin, Pooh himself does not live in a tree. The map shows him sitting on a log in front of quite an ordinary-looking front door. In the chapter on the flood, which we examined recently, we learn that he took refuge on the branch of a tree, which, in some editions, a large color picture locates just outside his door. What is the symbolic and Druidic meaning of this?

More clearly than words, the pictures tell us that Pooh is closely related to the trees but yet preserves a certain detachment from them. This aptly symbolizes his position. He is in his world yet not wholly of it. Hearing right at the beginning that he lives all by himself, we might label him a recluse. Yet no one is more sociable. Beautiful and satisfying though his world is, it cannot entirely contain him. He transcends it, as he transcends everything else. No category or description can confine him.

Similarly with trees. Pooh Bear is not in one but he lives close to one. We have seen it serve as a temporary dwelling during the flood. Though this was an emergency refuge, the picture shows Pooh sitting on a stout branch, accompanied by ten pots of honey. It conveys unmistakably the feeling that Pooh, despite the flood and the driving rain, is perfectly at ease in the tree. That is, it illustrates the relation between Bear and tree that proves him a true Druid.

The Problem of Identifying Trees in the World of Pooh

This picture also raises an interesting question. The combination of the ten pots of honey and a tree will spontaneously remind any Druidic student of the Celtic god Dagda. Dagda possessed the Cauldron of Plenty and he was the god of the Oak. Can we say then that

Pooh with his honey pots here symbolizes Dagda and the Cauldron of Plenty? What hinders us from an unqualified "Yes" is the nature of the tree. Is it an oak? No leaves appear either in this picture or in the earlier picture of it outside Pooh's front door. The branch and trunk seem too smooth for an oak, and look more like a beech. What is the solution to this mystery?

Five possible solutions leap immediately to mind. Let us follow Rabbit's example and tabulate them methodically. Numbers one to four I will give at once. The fifth I will postpone, for reasons that will become obvious very shortly.

1. We can dismiss as self-evidently absurd the suggestion that no symbolic meaning is present. This would simply be to fail to understand the nature of the

work we are studying, where everything has multiple symbolic meanings.

2. Equally absurd is the suggestion that either writer or artist made a mistake. This totally misconceives the nature of a text so manifestly inspired by the Inner Planes, which do not err.

3. Could the explanation be that we are faced with one of those "blinds" or deliberately misleading statements which some esoteric writers have used to hide deep truths from the uninitiated? This sounds more plausible but on reflection we must dismiss it. It is all too true that the Pooh opus has been, until recently, almost entirely misread, but this has always been due to the blindness of scholars, never to deliberate obfuscation by writer or artist.

4. Perhaps we have an allusion to the theory that the Achaeans, like the ancient Franks, had consulted beech oracles before they settled in Greece, where they substituted oaks for the beeches they could not find in their new home. The stimulating but unreliable Robert Graves rejects this theory but mentions that "beech" is etymologically connected with "book" and thus represents literature. It would be characteristic of our author to remind the initiated readers that they are studying a major work of literature, while the uninitiated fondly suppose they are merely reading a fantasy for children.

Confident that the explanation lies somewhere in the text itself, let us turn back to the beginning of Pooh's first recorded encounter with a tree. This occurs in Chapter One, "In Which We Are Introduced to Winnie-the-Pooh."

"One day when he was out walking, he came to an open place in the middle of the forest, and in the middle of this place was a large oak-tree . . ."

Here the text admits of no doubt. We have the plain words of the author himself that the tree is an oak. Yet the leaves are clearly not oak leaves. So now we come to the fifth suggested solution.

5. Perhaps the tree is not meant to represent a particular kind of tree but rather the Archetypal Tree. This is by far the most attractive solution yet. The Archetypal is thoroughly at home in the world of the Ancient Mysteries. Many well versed in esoteric symbolism are inclined to dismiss empirical detail when weighed against spiritual generalization.

Nevertheless, I am reluctant to accept this solution. My researches have taught me that Milne and Shepard are distinguished as much for precision of detail as for depth of meaning.

What, then, must we conclude? I suggest we should all give ourselves to prolonged meditation on these symbolic pictures or icons, as we might call them. The deepest students of the Ancient Mysteries assure us that such meditation will reveal truths incommunicable on the narrowly intellectual level of the written or spoken word. I shall be interested to hear from any reader who pursues this truly esoteric—and Druidic— path of investigation.

Passing on from the problematic nature of tree specification, we notice the important fact that as Pooh climbed what Milne certainly called an oak, he sang a little song. In a Druidic context, this clearly exemplifies one of the chief functions of a Druid: to be Bard.

Pooh as a Bard

Traditionally, Druids were divided into three main groups: Bards, Ovates (diviners) and Druids in the specialized sense. Writing in the first century B.C., the geographer Strabo said, "The Bards are singers and poets; the (O)vates diviners and natural philosophers; while the Druids, in addition to natural philosophy, study also moral philosophy."

On the whole, it is better to think of these three names as applying to functions rather than to separate groups. Even better, perhaps we should remember that to qualify finally as a Druid, a man or woman had to pass through the stages of Bard and Ovate on the way.

Pooh, as we should expect, was expert in all three functions.

By now, I daresay my readers are not surprised to hear that the Hums of Pooh have not been widely recognized as Bardic songs. Obviously, a complete Bardic analysis of the Hums of Pooh would take a massive volume in itself. We must content ourselves with a few brief comments.

Both its placing as the first Ursinian song and its special relation to the oak make the "little song" just referred to particularly important. Milne reports:

> *It went like this:*
> *Isn't it funny*
> *How a bear likes honey?*
> *Buzz! Buzz! Buzz!*
> *I wonder why he does?*

At the most casual glance, we notice that these four short lines contain two question marks and three exclamation marks. (Another whole volume could most profitably be devoted to the study of Milnean punctuation.) The punctuation here powerfully evokes a sense of wonder at the mysteries of nature and a desire to question them—reverently but profoundly. These are some of the Druid characteristics that strongly attract followers in our own era. We cannot doubt it is one of the many secrets of Pooh's lasting popularity, even among those who are quite unconscious of its deepest causes.

When we turn from our primarily visual impression, we find it is strongly reinforced by the text. The word "funny" is the very word to convey to Milne's ostensible audience of children a sense of strangeness. It suggests a mystery that cries out for solution. The "wonder" in the last line is self-explanatory. Its very transparency reinforces the message. Hardly less obvious is the empathy created in the second and third lines. The song does not merely talk about bears and bees: It enters into the ursine and apian natures. With Pooh himself, this is self-evident, but the triple onomatopoeia of "Buzz! Buzz! Buzz!" evokes beeness with equal vividness.

Having stimulated the sense of wonder and the urge to explore the mysteries of nature, Pooh, in the true tradition of the best spiritual guides, warns the aspirant that the quest is arduous and sometimes dangerous. As he climbs the tree in search of the honey of truth, even he feels weariness. His Complaining Song— ". . . (if the Bees were Bears), / We shouldn't have to climb up all these stairs"—stresses the difficulties, and his subsequent fall demonstrates the dangers. His own fall, of course, is planned and controlled, like the demonstration of a judo breakfall by a Black Belt. It does, however, show that a beginner might be in serious danger.

We content ourselves with a few brief comments on other examples of Pooh's Bardic songs. His *Tra-la-la, tra-la-la,/Tra-la-la, tra-la-la* has been widely misunderstood. There is really no excuse for this. Milne goes out of his way to signpost its importance. Chapter Two of *Winnie-the-Pooh* begins "Edward Bear, known to his friends as Winnie-the-Pooh, or Pooh for short . . ." That is, he reminds us of the crucial distinction between "Edward Bear," the name and so the aspect known to the profane vulgar, and "Winnie-the-Pooh," the name and aspect known to the initiates. He also mentions "Pooh for short," to remind us that within the circle of the initiates, there are different grades. "Pooh for short" implies the intimacy of those who have progressed beyond the first grade of initiation. The vigilant reader will notice that here he does not mention "Winnie-ther-Pooh," that name used only in the innermost and highest grades.

Having alerted his readers to the fact that they are now in the esoteric realm, Milne must have felt confident he could rely on their picking up the clear Druidic importance of the statement that Pooh "was walking through the *forest*" (my emphasis). Moreover, he was "humming proudly to himself." What could be more fraught with arcane significance than a Bardic song of which Pooh was consciously proud?

To make his meaning clearer still, Milne describes the precise circumstances in which Pooh had received his inspiration.

> *He had made up a little hum that very morning, as he was doing his Stoutness Exercises in front of the glass:* Tra-la-la, tra-la-la, *as he stretched up as high as he could go, and then* Tra-la-la, tra-la—oh, help!—la, *as he tried to reach his toes.*

This emphasis on poetic composition combined with physical exercise vividly symbolizes the Druidic union of the spiritual with the material. If doubt remains, just reflect on the significance of Pooh's stretching up as high as possible and then trying to reach his toes. This clearly symbolizes the reaching for the spiri-

tual heights and then trying to keep in touch with the earthly foundation. Normally, Pooh had no difficulty in keeping in touch with both poles of existence. His difficulty here doubtless arises from the timing. It is difficult to be intimately earthly at the very moment one is receiving input from the higher spheres.

Pooh's Major Epic

My last detailed comment on Pooh as Bard will refer, as my readers will doubtless expect, to his poetic celebration of Piglet's heroic deliverance of Owl—and Pooh himself. The title of Chapter Eight of *The House At Pooh Corner* prepares us for an outstandingly noble exploit: "In Which Piglet Does a Very Grand Thing."

Owl had just begun the story of what happened to his uncle Robert on a blusterous day, when a possibly even more blusterous day laid Owl tree house on the ground and blocked his front door, thus trapping him and his two guests, Pooh and Piglet. When Piglet realized the situation, he asked Owl how they were to get out.

"That is the problem, Piglet, to which I am asking Pooh to give his mind."

Note the significance of Owl's answer. Owl is obviously the representative of the academic intellect, with its strengths and perhaps its attendant limitations. It is therefore a particular pleasure to point out the perceptiveness with which he recognized the superior wisdom of Pooh and magnanimity with which he acknowledged it. What a lesson for all academics! Would that they too would recognize there are realms of wisdom beyond academia, and on occasion learn from poets and mystics.

Pooh immediately answers Owl's appeal. He explains that Piglet, who was, as we all know, a Very Small Animal, could be pulleyed up to Owl's letter-box, which was now above them. Then Piglet could—again because he was a Very Small Animal—crawl through the letter-box and make his way to other helpers. In the true spirit of a Druid guiding his community, Pooh formed this brilliant plan.

Though brilliant, it was not without danger for Piglet. Now, Druidic functions included inspiring valor

before an ordeal and the specifically Bardic function of celebrating heroic deeds and recording them for posterity. Pooh does both. First, he encourages the naturally somewhat nervous Piglet:

"... *if you save us all, it will be a Very Grand Thing to talk about afterwards, and perhaps I'll make up a Song, and people will say 'It was so grand what Piglet did that a Respectful Pooh Song was made about it.'"*

We read that "Piglet felt much better after this." And he carried out his heroic rescue. In due course, Pooh performed the celebratory Bardic function and recited the Respectful Pooh Song to Piglet. Over and above its poetic merits, two points are especially noteworthy. First, the number of verses:

"There are seven verses in it."
"Seven?" said Piglet as carelessly as he could. "You don't often get seven *verses in a Hum, do you, Pooh?"*
"Never," said Pooh. "I don't suppose it's ever *been heard of before."*

Seven is one of the great mystic numbers of the world. Moreover, it is announced three times. Three, of course, is another mystic number. The number seven stated three times gives a very special power indeed, and prepares us for the second esoteric element in this Hum. Meditating his promised song:

"But it isn't Easy," said Pooh to himself, as he looked at what had once been Owl's House. "Because Poetry and Hums aren't things which you get, they're things which get you. And all you can do is go where they can find you."

He waited hopefully. . . .

"Well," said Pooh after a long wait, "I shall begin 'Here lies a tree . . .'"

When he has finished and sung the song *three* times, he comments, "It's come different from what I thought it would, but it's come." We note the emphasis on inspiration. The Pooh corpus shows Pooh is an experienced Bard and master of many varied metrical forms. Yet here, on the verge of his greatest epic, he proclaims the need for the help of more mystical powers. He also tells us that the powers that inspire Hums have to be sought in the proper environment: "where they can find you." In our present Druidic context, it is inevitable that the great Respectful Pooh Song finds him in trees. He begins by tuning in to the "voice" of Owl's fallen chestnut tree. This brings the first inspiration, *"Here lies a tree."* Now fully open to the Muse, Pooh records all seven complex stanzas: a superb example of that combination of severely trained metrical expertise with arboreal inspiration and traditionally heroic subject matter, a combination which is archetypally Druidic.

Nor is this the end of it. Where is the chosen spot for Pooh as Bard to recite his epic to Piglet, its hero? Of course: when "they were walking back to the Hundred Acre Wood."

Pooh as Diviner (Ovate in Druidic Terms)

We read earlier that Ovates or Vates were "diviners and natural philosophers." We have already met Pooh as diviner or finder of lost or hidden objects: Eeyore's tail, for example, or the way home when Rabbit had lost them in the mist. Similarly, it is naturally Pooh who finds the North Pole. These examples are so obvious that even the most casual reader must register the bare facts, while the more perceptive will understand their meaning. So now I will analyze a more obscure and subtle example, which seems so far to have escaped notice. I refer to the search for Small.

Rabbit asks Pooh to join the search for Small, one of Rabbit's friends-and-relations, who is missing. Pooh agrees, saying good-bye affectionately to the honey pots he has been counting. Immediately we notice his active benevolence. In a truly Druidic spirit, he abandons his personal concerns to devote himself to the good of the community.

As soon as Rabbit was out of sight, Pooh remembered that he had forgotten to ask who Small was, and whether he was the sort of friend-and-relation who settled on one's nose, or the sort who got trodden on by mistake . . .

To help his task, he makes an

ORDER OF LOOKING FOR THINGS

1. *Special Place.* (To find Piglet.)
2. *Piglet.* (To find who Small is.)
3. *Small.* (To find Small.)
4. *Rabbit.* (To tell him I've found Small.)
5. *Small Again.* (To tell him I've found Rabbit.)

Then, "because Pooh was so busy not looking where he was going that he stepped on a piece of the Forest which had been left out by mistake," he fell into a pit and landed on top of Piglet. After some conversation not relevant to our present purpose, Piglet sees Small—a Very Small Beetle—climbing up Pooh's back. The search is over.

Now, I am confident that the readers who have followed me so far would not for a moment suppose this episode shows Pooh as an uncomprehending, absent-minded blunderer who stumbles on the object of his search by accident. They may, however, hold on to the truth of this by faith rather than by rational inference from concrete evidence, so I will point out the evidence and draw the inescapable logical conclusion.

One of the recurrent themes of *Pooh and the Ancient Mysteries* is the superiority of intuitive wisdom to superficial rationality. At this point, therefore, some readers may accuse me of paradox, even of self-contradiction. How, they may ask, how can you proclaim the superiority of intuition when you have just promised to validate your interpretation of the text by such rationalistic means as concrete evidence and logical inference?

The explanation, as it is so often, is a matter of different levels. At the appropriate level—the level of everyday life—concrete evidence and rigorous logic have their proper place; and it is a most valuable one. It is at this rational level that I am now interpreting the text. And what could be more valuable than that? The text clearly points out that the Way exists. I merely indicate that it does so. Following the Way is a matter of choice and experience. The difference is parallel to, though much greater than, the difference between the intellectual effort of tracing a route on the map and the experiential effort of travelling that route oneself. Having, I trust, put my critics' minds at rest, I return to the exegesis of the text.

Throughout the search for Small, we must imagine Pooh's attitude as one of benevolent detachment, indulging Rabbit's bureaucratic "organdizing" of everybody, but with a quiet smile to himself. If we had any doubts about this, two pieces of evidence would remove them. Pooh says he will have to look for Piglet in the Special Place first. "I wonder where it is." Now, if there was one thing that Druids knew profoundly, it was the whereabouts and nature of Special Places. Pooh must really have been wondering whether a Rabbit-organized Special Place was truly Special.

Secondly, his Order of Looking for Things is clearly a parody of Rabbit's PLAN TO CAPTURE BABY ROO. This, as all Ursinologists will remember, consisted of eleven numbered sections, beginning—

1. *General Remarks.* Kanga runs faster than any of Us, even Me.
2. *More General Remarks.* Kanga never takes her eye off Baby Roo, except when he's safely buttoned up in her pocket.
3. *Therefore.* If we are to capture Baby Roo, we must get a Long Start, because Kanga runs faster than any of Us, even Me. *(See 1.)*

No one who remembers this could possibly take Pooh's list as more than his little joke. We were all sure from the beginning that it was no accident that associated Piglet so closely with the search for Small. Our confidence is amply rewarded when it is Piglet who sees and recognizes Small on Pooh's back. I think we must assume that by this time Pooh has inwardly chosen Piglet for his future disciple. It would clearly strain coincidence to the breaking point to suggest that mere chance brought first Piglet and then Pooh to fall into the very pit where Small was to be found. Finding lost persons, objects and routes is only one of the ways in which Pooh Bear exercised the Druidic function of helping the community of his friends in the Forest. Doubtless we could all remember many similar instances, but mere accumulation would miss the point. They are simply examples of a central guiding power. In the Druid solar tradition, this is symbolized by Pooh's close relations with the sun. Just as the sun gives light, warmth and life to our world, so does Winnie-ther-Pooh—only his full, mystical title will do here—so does he light, warm and vivify the World of Pooh.

Pooh as a Natural Philosopher

The search for Small also shows us Pooh exercising the third Druidic function: the function of a Natural

Philosopher, which, until fairly recent times, meant a scientist.

When Pooh falls into the pit, note the scientific curiosity with which he examines his own physical responses during this startling and potentially dangerous experience.

"I'm flying. What Owl does. I wonder how you stop—" when he stopped.

Puzzled by squeaks from the still unseen Piglet,

"That's funny," thought Pooh. "I said 'Ow!' without really oo'ing."
"Help!" said a small, high voice.
"That's me again," thought Pooh. "I've had an Accident, and fallen down a well, and my voice has gone all squeaky and works before I'm ready for it, because I've done something to myself inside. Bother!"

A little later he diagnoses "A Very Bad Accident to Pooh Bear." He still remains calm. Druidic science importantly included medicine, so it is not surprising to find Pooh observing his own symptoms with the scientific detachment of a medical experimenter.

The Great Feasts of the Druid Calendar

Much writing about these feasts is highly speculative. There is, in fact, little evidence of pre-Christian rituals in the British Isles. As Pooh transcends the ordinary boundaries of space and time, I feel justified in drawing on all Druidic sources, ancient and modern, British, Irish and Continental, in this chapter. This applies particularly to what modern Druids consider the great solar feasts of the Druid calendar: the midsummer and midwinter solstices, and the spring and autumn equinoxes.

Pooh's close relationship with the sun has already been amply demonstrated. It is equally obvious that he celebrates midwinter by "a Good Hum, such as is Hummed Hopefully to Others." He emphasizes his joy in this feast by repeating the song to Piglet while they complete the ritual by walking out together in the snow. As he explains to the somewhat unenthusiastic Piglet, "It's a special Outdoor Song which Has To Be Sung In The Snow." It is natural that Pooh should experience particular pleasure in the winter solstice, as traditionally it was celebrated at night, lit chiefly by the stars of the Great Bear.

One morning when Pooh visits Piglet, he finds him digging and asks what he is doing. "I'm planting an acorn, Pooh, so that it can grow up into an oak-tree."

This is clearly a springtime activity, and therefore

refers to the celebration of the spring equinox. Significantly, it is an oak that Piglet hopes to grow. After these two brief references, the text treats the autumn equinox at much greater length.

> *One day, when Pooh was walking towards this bridge, he was trying to make up a piece of poetry about fir-cones, because there they were, lying about on each side of him, and he felt singy. So he picked a fir-cone up, and looked at it, and said to himself, "This is a very good fir-cone, and something ought to rhyme to it." But he couldn't think of anything. And then this came into his head suddenly:*
>
>> *Here is a myst'ry*
>> *About a little fir-tree.*
>> *Owl says it's his tree,*
>> *And Kanga says it's her tree.*
>
> *"Which doesn't make sense," said Pooh, "because Kanga doesn't live in a tree."*

This short passage is so packed with Druidic meanings that it will take longer to analyze than to quote. Fir-cones are, of course, characteristic of autumn and I need not labor the reference to that season. This passage also emphasizes their rich plentifulness: "there they were, lying about on each side of him." "Season of cones and mellow fruitfulness," as Keats so neatly wrote. Profoundly in tune with Nature—another Druidic trait—Pooh feels poetic inspiration rising in him: "he felt singy . . . But he couldn't think of anything. And then this came into his head suddenly."

The first two lines that came into his head salute the "very good fir-cone": Clearly, it was a fit representative of the creative mystery it embodied. The next two lines recognize that such different beings as Owl and Kanga share in the universal creativity Pooh is singing about. His apparently dismissive comment that Kanga doesn't live in a tree forestalls an unenlightened objection by explaining that the fir-tree is Owl's and Kanga's, not in the sense that they literally possess it, but in the deeper sense that they all share in it as part of what Shakespeare called "great creating Nature."

We note in passing that while Pooh was celebrating the autumn equinox by hymning the fir-cone, he was also about to use that same cone to initiate the game of Poohsticks, an interesting substitute for the yarrow stalks traditionally used to tap the eastern wisdom of the I-Ching. Yet another example of his universal genius.

These Druidic festivals strongly emphasize the close communion of the Druid with Nature; something most subtly displayed by Pooh in the attempted unbouncing of Tigger. When Rabbit announces his plan for unbouncing Tigger, "It was a drowsy summer afternoon, and the Forest was full of gentle sounds, which all seemed to be saying to Pooh, 'Don't listen to Rabbit, listen to me.' So he got into a comfortable position for not listening to Rabbit."

Throughout the whole episode, Pooh continues in the same attitude of detached neutrality. He accompanies his friends on the unbouncing expedition but, unusually for him, takes no active part. Why? Because he foresees the failure of Rabbit's plan? No doubt he does, but, much more importantly, because he respects Tigger's essential nature and would not want to see it unnaturally tamed. His attitude is clearly at one with Milne's when the latter describes "a Tigger who bounced, if he bounced at all, in just the beautiful way a Tigger ought to bounce."

The Druidic Meaning of "The Brain of Pooh"

Of course, when we read the Pooh cycle, we meet Pooh already initiated into the highest grade of Druidry, but

he does remind us of the most testing of the initiations he must have passed through on the way. Even those who know nothing of Druid lore must have experienced a haunting sense of some deeper meaning when they read the passage where Pooh inverts Christopher Robin's umbrella and they sail together to rescue the flood-bound Piglet.

The two drawings of the craft are even more evocative than the words. Can we read those words and examine those pictures without thinking of the coracle, the circular boat of the Ancient Britons? Equally inevitably, given our present topic, we remember that Taliesin, that initiate Bard, describes being put out to sea in an open boat as the supreme test of the candidate for the highest mysteries. Truly, Christopher Robin was inspired when he uttered the words, "I shall call this boat *The Brain of Pooh*."

In the course of this chapter, we have seen Pooh as a Druid of the highest order: showing active goodwill to

the community of the Forest; using his divinatory powers for his friends; demonstrating a beneficent purpose
underlying apparent chance; and, especially, advancing
the preparation of his chosen disciple, Piglet.

Remembering all this, we cannot doubt that
William Blake's prophetic vision included Winnie-the-
Pooh when he wrote:

> *O hear the voice of the Bard*
> *Who present, past and future sees,*
> *Whose ears have heard the holy word*
> *That walked among the ancient Trees.*

7

POOH AND THE ARTHURIAN MYSTERIES

Christopher Robin as King Arthur

So far, Christopher Robin has not played a very impressive part in our studies. Amiable, honorable and courteous he undoubtedly is, but his repeated failure to appreciate the profound wisdom of Winnie-the-Pooh shows his narrow limits, spiritually and intellectually. So I am happy to announce that in this chapter he comes into his own. As we shall see, in an Arthurian context, Pooh represents Merlin. Now, if Pooh is Merlin, who is Arthur? It can only be Christopher Robin. Christopher Robin's limitations, of course, confirm the analogy between him and King Arthur. Arthur too was honorable, courteous and well-meaning. His judgment, though, was often faulty. On many occasions, only Merlin's advice saved him from disaster.

Christopher Robin demonstrates his Arthurian role unmistakably when he inspires the Expotition to the North Pole. He not only inspires it, he leads it in person. By doing so, he combines the earlier with the later stories of Arthur. For the first accounts show King Arthur leading his people in the field, whereas the later ones show him sending his knights forth on their quests, while he remains at court.

We find a further striking detail of Christopher Robin's Arthurian role as he is preparing for the Expotition to the North Pole. When Pooh visits him on that very special morning,

Christopher Robin was sitting outside his door, putting on his Big Boots. As soon as he saw the Big Boots, Pooh knew that an Adventure was going to happen.

Clearly the Big Boots represent the armor that the king donned before setting out on an adventure. Per-

haps also they remind us of the Seven-League Boots in other tales, and so hint at his horse. We cannot fail to notice that Christopher Robin needs Pooh's help to get his boots on. Pooh thus doubles the exoteric and comparatively humble office of squire with the esoteric, powerful role of Merlin, who made Arthur's successes possible.

Throughout the Expotition, Christopher Robin sustains the role of a good general. He does not need Napoleon to teach him that an army marches on its stomach: He announces to Pooh, "And we must all bring Provisions." He is at once prudent—"we're just coming to a Dangerous Place," he warns his followers— and bold—fearlessly, he leads them through it. He displays a proper regard for the well-being of his followers. Once the Dangerous Place had been passed, they reached "a level strip of grass on which they could sit down and rest." Then, "I think," said Christopher Robin, "that we ought to eat all our Provisions now, so that we shan't have so much to carry."

Finally, when they reach the North Pole and Pooh discovers it, Christopher Robin shows a suitably royal generosity in recognizing and rewarding the discoverer. Of course, to those of us who know Pooh's true nature, there is something richly ironic in the spectacle of the amiable but limited Christopher Robin assuming a benevolent superiority to the Bear of Enormous Brain.

However, we must acknowledge that he was doing his best according to his lights.

Many references show that the other Forest-dwellers regard Christopher Robin as fulfilling the proper kingly function of a benevolent protector, whom they turn to for help. As early as Chapter Two of *Winnie-the-Pooh*, when Pooh is stuck in Rabbit's doorway, Rabbit says, "Well, well, I shall go and fetch Christopher Robin." When Roo is kidnapped, Kanga immediately comforts herself: "for she felt quite sure that Christopher Robin would never let any harm happen to Roo."

Even at his most timid, "Piglet wasn't afraid if he had Christopher Robin with him." Piglet's hero worship of Christopher Robin illuminates an important detailed Arthurian identification. Christopher Robin, performing the Arthurian function of rescuing Tigger and Roo from the tree where Tigger's rashness has marooned them, announces his plan.

"I'll take off my tunic and we'll each hold a corner, and then Roo and Tigger can jump into it, and it will be all soft and bouncy for them, and they won't hurt themselves."

. . . But Piglet wasn't listening, he was so agog at the thought of seeing Christopher Robin's blue braces again. He had only seen them once before, when he was

much younger, and, being a little over-excited by them, had had to go to bed half an hour earlier than usual; and he had always wondered since if they were really as blue and bracing as he had thought them.

The very special emphasis on the blueness of Christopher Robin's braces points unmistakably to some major significance. In an Arthurian context, this can only be to the blue riband of the Order of the Garter, which was a conscious medieval revival of the Knights of the Round Table. When King Edward III instituted the Order of the Garter in 1348, it was with the express, indeed oath-bound, intention of following in the footsteps of King Arthur and creating a Round Table for his own knights.

The Round Table

This is all very well, some readers may be thinking, but what about the Round Table itself? Surely that is an essential part of the Arthurian picture, yet it appears nowhere in any of the Shepard drawings. The nearest parallel to one of the great feasts of the Round Table is the party that Christopher Robin gave to celebrate Pooh's rescue of Piglet from the flood. Yet, if we look at the picture, we see the shape is uncompromisingly oblong. How do we explain this?

One might be tempted to reply that Shepard's tables, like some of his other pictures, should be interpreted symbolically. No doubt this is true as far as it goes, but it feels perhaps a little glib. Satisfactory symbols are always imaginatively related to whatever they symbolize. We must look for something better than a vague invocation of a dubiously justified symbol. Those familiar with the *Transcendental Magic* of Eliphas Levi will not have far to look. Levi cites a "Hebrew manuscript of the sixteenth century" to the effect that an accomplished Magus will be able to square the circle. So now we see that the puzzling angular tables are simply examples of this acknowledged magical power.

Pooh as Merlin

Even before I mentioned the fact, I am sure my readers intuitively recognized Winnie-the-Pooh as the representative of Merlin in the Arthurian myth. Right from the beginning, Milne takes special care to alert us to this identification. Long before it is clear, he prepares us by several hints whose full meaning is revealed later. The multiplicity of names—Edward Bear, Winnie-ther-Pooh, Pooh, Pooh Bear—precisely parallels the fact that the oldest references to Merlin call him Lailoken or Laloecen or Lallogan and then Myrddin.

As early as Chapter Two of *Winnie-the-Pooh*, we read that Pooh was "walking gaily along, wondering what everybody else was doing, and what it felt like, being somebody else." In isolation, we might take this as simply another example of Pooh's wide-ranging mind. Thinking of Merlin, however, we interpret it as referring to Merlin's powers as a master of magical disguise: a shape-shifter, in the technical jargon. These powers are often recorded in Arthurian tales. When, for example, he first revealed the secret of Arthur's birth, Arthur did not believe him because Merlin had appeared "lyke a chylde of fourtene yere of ayge."

Rather surprisingly, it is Rabbit who is most aware of shape-shifting. He even tries it himself. When Pooh visits him in Chapter Two of *Winnie-the-Pooh,* Rabbit first denies there is anybody at home. When Pooh asks,

> *"Hallo, Rabbit, isn't that you?"*
> *"No," said Rabbit, in a different sort of voice this time.*
> *"But isn't that Rabbit's voice?"*
> *"I don't think so," said Rabbit. "It isn't meant to be."*

Then, when Pooh announces himself, "But this *is* Me!" Rabbit asks, "What sort of Me?" This otherwise rather cryptic dialogue becomes quite clear as soon as we see that Rabbit was trying what we might call oral shape-shifting himself. His attempt was only partially successful, as Pooh's recognition of Rabbit's voice shows. Finally, Rabbit's question—what sort of Me is there?—implies previous knowledge of Pooh's shape-shifting.

Both Merlin and Arthur had distinctly irregular births, and Pooh and Piglet show exquisite tact in alerting the initiated while avoiding anything unsuitable for a child in the 1920s. When Piglet talks about his grandfather, Trespassers W, Pooh wonders what a grandfather was like. This absence of a normal ancestry is the nearest Milne could get in a children's story to the account in Geoffrey of Monmouth's medieval best-seller, *The*

History of the Kings of Britain. He told his readers that Merlin had been fathered by an incubus (a sexually potent male demon) on a nun. Merlin's diabolical fatherhood is counteracted with the help of his mother's confessor, and his supernatural powers are employed in good causes. Naturally and rightly, it is solely this side of him that Pooh represents.

The same conventions inhibited any reference to Arthur's conception, which Merlin contrived by magically disguising Arthur's predecessor, King Uther Pendragon, as Gorlois, Duke of Cornwall, so that he might lie with Gorlois' wife, Ygerne, in Tintagel Castle. When Gorlois was killed in battle, Uther married Ygerne. When Arthur was born of this union, it was Merlin who received the infant, handed him over to a foster father, Sir Ector, and later arranged for him to be recognized as the true King of England, successfully guiding him till his kingship was firmly established.

So far at least, I have not been able to trace parallels to every detail of this complicated tale. All that we can confidently transfer from it to the World of Pooh is that, in some mysterious way, Pooh Bear has a guiding and perhaps quasi-parental influence on the development of Christopher Robin.

The social context of the Pooh books precludes overt guidance of Christopher Robin by Pooh. However, we cannot doubt that Christopher Robin's gradual

maturing is due to the covert but powerful influence of
Pooh Bear. For, limited though Christopher Robin's
scope is, it is perfectly suited to his vocation in life. He
is, as we saw long ago, not the stuff of which a Magus is
made; profound wisdom and occult knowledge would
be wasted in the everyday world which is his destined
sphere. There, his qualities of amiability, courtesy and
honor would be invaluable. Both his goodwill and his
sublime incomprehension appear in the last chapter of
The House At Pooh Corner, when he dubs the Great
Bear a knight.

   The irony of this scene encapsulates the oft repeated situation when some well-meaning mediocrity
representing political power condescends to bestow a
trivial honor on genius. To do Christopher Robin justice, he does show some awareness of what he is about

to lose when he departs, not, like Arthur, "to the island-valley of Avilion," but to a world of "Factors . . . Suction Pumps . . . and what comes from Brazil," a world where "they don't let you . . . do Nothing any more."

Happily, this is not the end. Just as Arthur is "the once and future king," who will come again to his king-dom, so we read: "But wherever they go, and whatever happens to them on the way, in that enchanted place on the top of the Forest, a little boy and his Bear will always be playing." Pooh himself, of course, remains forever in his own World. If Christopher Robin's im-mediate future is duller than Arthur's, Pooh's is much happier than Merlin's. Merlin, you will remember, is usually supposed to have been magically imprisoned by the Lady of the Lake. Far from being imprisoned by a powerful enchantress, Pooh forms a happy friendship with the only female in the cycle. At the end of Chapter Seven of *Winnie-the-Pooh,* we read that "every Tuesday Kanga spent the day with her great friend Pooh, teach-ing him to jump." It is significant that she taught him to *jump,* a liberating and elevating activity, exactly contrary to imprisonment.

The Quest: An Arthurian Theme in Ursinian Terms

The Round Table naturally leads us to the theme of the Quest. It was from the Round Table that so many of the knights set forth on their separate adventures. Milne, always faithful to the spirit rather than the letter, felt free to vary the starting point of his questors.

The Quest for the Heffalump, in Chapter Five of *Winnie-the-Pooh,* begins when Christopher Robin raises the subject of Heffalumps while he is picnicking with Pooh and Piglet. There are two obvious difficulties in taking this quest quite seriously. In the first place, none of the three speakers brings really convincing evidence that he has actually seen a Heffalump. Christopher Robin says he has but is remarkably vague about what it is. Piglet says he saw one once—"At least, I think I did. . . . Only perhaps it wasn't." Pooh wonders what a Heffalump is like. Their accounts may converge but they hardly convince.

Second, Pooh's plan for trapping one is so absurd as to be an obvious joke. Can we believe that the Great Brain would really hope that a Heffalump would fall into a trap because it would be looking up either to see if it would rain or to see if it would stop raining? Remembering that Piglet was still at an early stage of his training, we can understand that Pooh was simply giving his little disciple an object lesson in the need to make thorough investigations before committing himself to a quest. This also explains the earlier mystifying statement that Pooh wondered what a Heffalump was like. If Pooh did not know what a Heffalump was like, the most probable explanation was that no such thing as a Heffalump existed: It was as unknown to mythology as to zoology.

Equally elusive was the quarry in Chapter Three of *Winnie-the-Pooh,* "In Which Pooh and Piglet Go Hunting and Nearly Catch a Woozle." The most remarkable feature of this chase was the way in which the quarry's tracks first doubled and were then joined by a third set which made different marks. As Pooh explains,

"It is either Two Woozles and one, as it might be, Wizzle, or Two, as it might be, Wizzles and one, if so it is, Woozle."

Soon after, they find the tracks of another Woozle in front of them. No one familiar with Malory's *Morte D'Arthur* can fail to see the reference to the occasion when King Arthur saw the Questing Beast: He "thought he herde a noyse of howundis [hounds] to the som [sum] of thirty and with that the kynge saw com towarde hym the strongeste beste [strangest beast] that he ever saw or herde of." The multiplication of the tracks in Pooh's quest brilliantly hints at mysterious numbers while making it possible to explain them in a manner both plausible and amusing.

Christopher Robin had been watching Pooh and Piglet from a branch above. He explained the increase in the tracks as merely the result of the questors' circling round and round the spinney, and making a different set of tracks at each circuit. Pooh accepts this easy explanation, and even reproaches himself: " 'I have been Foolish and Deluded,' said he, 'and I am a Bear of No Brain at All.' " Those who know more of the Questing Beast will remember that it was impossible to catch. On the spiritual level, it has been taken to symbolize questing for its own sake, without any rational or attainable object. Here, we see Pooh Bear sacrificing his own dignity to save his little friend from wasting his energies in a futile quest.

I feel that by now my readers may be getting impatient for the Ancient Mysteries, which are the proclaimed subject of this work. Surely, they may be saying to themselves, something more is needed than mere references to Merlin as a magician and some examples of shapeshifting. They are quite right, and now we are coming to the heart of the matter: the mystical meaning that underlies the ceremonial impressiveness of King Arthur's court and the chivalric adventures of his knights.

The World of Pooh and the Mystical Logres of Arthurian Legend

The World of Pooh demonstrates what has long been known to initiates: that underlying the actual realm of

Arthur was an ideal realm, often called Logres to distinguish it from the harsher reality of Britain. The esoteric aim of the king and his knights was to make the ideal real; to transform Britain into Logres.

They failed to bring the idyllic land of Logres into the material world. But where they failed, Winnie-ther-Pooh and his friends succeeded. Whatever else is debatable, in Arthurian terms, the World of Pooh is indubitably the Realm of Logres. It is a world of unruffled friendship, where such crises as do arise serve only to activate the practical benevolence of its dwellers, from the general search for Small to countless individual acts of hospitality, kindness and assistance. Unlike King Arthur, Christopher Robin has no rivals to threaten him, no treacherous Mordred to destroy him. Unlike Guinevere's, Kanga's reputation is not threatened by court scandals. No bitter feuds, like that between Lancelot and Gawain, divide the dwellers in the Forest.

This leads us to the occult explanation of the successful establishment of Logres in the World of Pooh compared with the failure to establish it in the Realm of Arthur. That well-known contemporary occult writer, Gareth Knight, argues that Arthur's failure was largely due to the fact that he never achieved a satisfactory relationship with Guinevere. Within the conventions of a children's story, the nearest Milne could approach to a marriage was a great friendship. We may conclude that the special friendship between Pooh and Kanga was both made possible by the happy state already existing in Pooh's World and also secured its foundations and continuance.

The North Pole and the Holy Grail

We have already dealt with the Expotition to the North Pole on the purely material level. Now we must examine it more deeply, as an example of the mystical meaning underlying the mere adventures that appear on the surface. It is precisely this mystical meaning that Winnie-the-Pooh illuminates. Without it, indeed, there would be no place for Arthurian Britain in the World of Pooh.

We are bound to compare it with the most important quest in Arthurian legend: the Quest for the Holy Grail. At first, the contrasts seem more striking than the similarities. The North Pole and the Holy Grail could hardly be more unlike. Moreover, Malory tells us that after the knights of the Round Table had vowed to undertake the quest for the Holy Grail, they set out together but then

. . . they were all accorded that they sholde departe everych from othir. And on the morne . . . every knyght toke the way that hym lyked beste.

Now we read

First came Christopher Robin and Rabbit, then Piglet and Pooh; then Kanga, with Roo in her pocket, and Owl; then Eeyore; and, at the end, in a long line, all Rabbit's friends-and-relations.

With the sole exception of that too timid questor, Alexander Beetle, they stay together until the end.

Finally, and most striking—of all the goodly fellowship of the Round Table, only three achieve the full vision of the Grail. Whereas all Christopher Robin's company—with that one exception—are present to see the North Pole, which, as we should expect, Winnie-the-Pooh discovers.

By now, I am confident that my readers have seen the obvious explanation. The success of the Quest for the North Pole is just what we should expect after seeing the Realm of Logres so triumphantly embodied in the World of Pooh. The link is equally obvious. The achievements of the three successful Grail knights—Sir Galahad, Sir Perceval and Sir Bors—brought appropriate rewards to those three individuals but failed to restore Logres. In the World of Pooh, Logres exists throughout in untroubled serenity. And it is in this world of mutual aid that the Quest for the North Pole achieves its natural triumph.

As much of this book deals with occult mysteries

outside the boundaries of accepted science, it is pleasing to record that the success of Christopher Robin's Expotition is soundly based on modern psychological research. Experimental psychologists have demonstrated the theory they call Social Facilitation. This proves that the individual members of a group operate more effectively together than when they are working entirely on their own. This applies even to that comparatively simpleminded creature, the wood louse. As I am always careful to avoid any kind of extravagant speculation, I must admit that our texts nowhere explicitly mention the wood louse, but there is little doubt that we should include it, with beetles and spiders, in the varied collection of Rabbit's friends-and-relations: one of those Pooh thought of as belonging to "the sort who got trodden on by mistake." Even the humblest of Rabbit's friends-and-relations played its part in facilitating the great discovery of the Great Bear.

At this stage, some readers may feel a slight uneasiness. They may wonder whether the North Pole is a satisfactory symbol for the Grail. True, ancient legends of the Grail present it in very varied guises: a chalice, a large dish, a cauldron, even a stone. Could it not therefore equally well appear as a pole? All the more as it gave the successful questors a satisfaction and a joy equivalent to that experienced by the traditional achievers of the Grail.

We can perhaps accept the Expotition as a perfect

symbol of the achieved quest. I think, however, we need to seek for a symbol of the Grail itself more concretely related to the traditional forms.

Fortunately, we have not far to seek.

Was Pooh's Jar of Hunny the Holy Grail?

Symbolically at least, the answer is a resounding Yes. Traditionally, Merlin was especially the prophet of the Grail, and Milne took particular care to emphasize the close connection between Pooh in his Merlin aspect and the symbols of the Holy Grail and its pre-Christian prototype, the Celtic Cauldron of Plenty.

Previous chapters have already shown that honey in the World of Pooh is a symbol of spiritual wisdom and occult lore. On the material plane too, Pooh is sustained for his active and energetic life by small quantities—"smackerels"—of this marvelous substance. All this echoes what such Arthurian authorities as Chrétien de Troyes and Sir Thomas Malory tell us of the miraculous sustaining powers of the Grail.

Pooh Bear himself emphasizes the purity and consistency of his jar of HUNNY. In Chapter Five of *Winnie-the-Pooh,* he subjects this jar, step by step, to the most searching tests. The jar is just where it should be: the top shelf of his larder; it has "HUNNY" written on it: "Just to make sure, he took off the paper cover and looked at it, and it *looked* just like honey." In his Merlin role, however, Pooh is well aware of magical shape-shifting and the illusions of gramarye. "So he put his tongue in, and took a large lick." Taste confirms place, label and sight. Still, with prudent caution, he tests and happily disconfirms the hypothesis that somebody might have put cheese at the bottom, "just for a joke." At last, he is able to say, "It *is* honey, right the way down."

No other writer has given his readers such convincing proofs of the true nature of the Grail and its co tents.

Some Ursinologists may be a little surprised at the repeated references to the number of Pooh's pots. They will remember that when Pooh took refuge from the flood, he took ten pots of honey with him. When Rabbit calls on Pooh to ask his help in the search for Small, Pooh is counting his pots of honey and had reached fourteen—or was it fifteen? Four chapters later, when Rabbit has lost himself and everybody else in the attempt to unbounce Tigger, it is the call of Pooh's twelve pots of honey that guides him and Piglet home.

These references are clear reminders of the pre-medieval and even pre-Christian origins from which so many of the familiar Arthurian tales are derived: The multiplicity of Pooh's honey pots plainly symbolizes the Celtic origins of the Grail as a Cauldron of Plenty. A cauldron of honey would be artistically inadmissible. A *number* of honey pots combines artistic decorum with a vision of lavish plenty. Nor is the pot of HUNNY Milne's only symbolic identification of Pooh with the Grail Keeper. Pooh's song "Cottleston Pie" tells us at the end of every verse—

> *Ask me a riddle and I reply:*
> "Cottleston, Cottleston, Cottleston Pie."

That is, Cottleston Pie satisfies every conceivable appetite of the mind, while the chosen metaphor allows, indeed encourages, us to take it as physically satisfying also. A perfect image of the all-nourishing contents of the Cauldron of Plenty.

Roo, Eeyore and Sir Perceval

In this short and elementary work, there is no time to point out the parallels between Pooh's friends and individual characters in Arthurian legend. I am happy to leave this to my readers, who will derive pleasure and profit from tracing these symbolic identifications: Rabbit, for example, with Sir Kay; Tigger with the Green Knight and—more remotely—with Sir Lancelot; Owl with the wise hermits who give sage advice to so many knights in distress. They will also notice that marked similarity between Galleons Lap, that part of the Forest Christopher Robin knew was enchanted, and the enchanted Forest of Broceliande in Arthurian legend.

One parallel, however, I will go into just a little further: the parallel of Roo with Perceval. When Roo wants to join the others who plan to unbounce Tigger, Kanga says,

> *"I think not today, dear. Another day."*
> *"Tomorrow?" said Roo hopefully.*
> *"We'll see," said Kanga.*
> *"You're always seeing, and nothing ever happens,"*
> *said Roo sadly.*

What is this but a restatement in terms appropriate to our text of the attempts Perceval's mother made to shield him from all knowledge of knightly adventures? The great twelfth-century Arthurian writer, Chrétien de Troyes, tells us that when Perceval told his mother of his thrilling first view of knights, "she said like a woman distraught: '. . . My dear, sweet son, I thought I could shield you so well from knighthood that you'd never hear of it.' "

Later, when Perceval first sees the Grail procession, he takes too literally the advice he had received not to talk too much, and so fails to ask the questions that would have healed both the wounded Fisher King and his kingdom. Even Eeyore is ahead of him here. At our very first meeting, he is at least asking questions: "Why?" "Wherefore?" "Inasmuch as which?" Another striking example of the lofty status of even the less obviously spiritual inhabitants of the World of Pooh as compared with one of the most successful Grail knights.

Questions proved a stumbling block both to Sir Perceval and to his son, the Grail Knight Lohengrin. Perceval erred by failing to ask the right question; Lohengrin by answering the wrong one. When he yielded to his wife's importunity and betrayed the mysterious secret of his true name and origin, he was punished by permanent separation from her; and was borne away—on a swan. This explains the vagueness of Milne's reference to a swan in his Introduction to *Winnie-the-Pooh* (see page 8). Remembering the fate of Lohengrin, our benevolent author was obviously warning us of the dangers of inappropriate demands for knowledge. Our next chapter will show that the Mysteries must be approached step by step. Patience is as necessary as perseverance.

8

POOH AS THE MYSTICAL
GUIDE OF HIS FRIENDS:

Initiatory Rites, Pooh as a Noah Figure

Several times and in very different contexts, we have glanced at the ways in which the benevolent Bear has helped his friends. So far we have dwelt mostly on examples of practical assistance, such as his restoring Eeyore's tail and rescuing Piglet from the flood. I am sure that many readers must be asking, But what about his spiritual assistance? Why did he choose Piglet as his disciple, or *chela*? And how did he influence the spiritual progress of his other friends?

Approaching these questions systematically, let us look first at those archetypal initiatory references that Milne has placed right at the beginning of the Work, then at a detailed analysis of Piglet's progress, and finally at the lesser but still praiseworthy advances of the others.

As the theme of initiation is so important in the Pooh cycle, it is not surprising that Milne signals it at the very beginning, in the Introduction to *Winnie-the-Pooh*. Like everything in these great texts, this can, and indeed should, be interpreted in many different ways and on many different levels. By now we can see at a glance that the reference to Pooh as a caged bear shows him enacting the role of a candidate for the Mysteries, still imprisoned in the darkness of ignorance. Initiation into the Mysteries is the essential first step into the light. As we might expect, we find a major symbolic passage devoted to this vital ceremony.

Few incidents in the life of Winnie-the-Pooh have been so grossly misunderstood as his visit to Rabbit, when he gets stuck in Rabbit's doorway on trying to leave. Almost universally, this incident has been taken as comic retribution for greed-induced fatness. It is little to the credit of previous Ursinologists that they have failed to see the obvious connection with the Eleusinian Mysteries.

Once again, Winnie-ther-Pooh, with typical humility, plays the role of initiate for our benefit. When Pooh goes visiting, he sees the entrance to Rabbit's burrow.

So he bent down, put his head into the hole, and called out:

"Is anybody at home?"

There was a sudden scuffling noise from inside the hole, and then silence.

"What I said was, 'Is anybody at home?' " called out Pooh very loudly.

"No!" said a voice; and then added, "you needn't shout so loud. I heard you quite well the first time."

At last, and only when careful questions have provisionally established Pooh's identity, does Rabbit acknowledge his own, and invite Pooh in. Even then, he inspects him carefully: "You were quite right," said Rabbit, looking at him all over. "It *is* you."

Here we have the typical features of entry into a Mystery cult, and the candidate's descent into a lower world, often a cave, reminds us of the Eleusinian Mysteries, the most famous of all such cults. Also typical is the Guardian of the Portal, who subjects the candidate to a searching examination before admitting him. As

Rabbit puts it: "One can't have *anybody* coming into one's house. One has to be *careful.*"

It may surprise some to find the Portal is guarded by Rabbit, who, despite many admirable qualities, does not impress us as one far advanced in the Mysteries. Let us remember, however, that though the Guardian of the Portal performs an essential function, he is quite often not an initiate of the innermost secrets of the shrine he guards.

Every Ursinologist will have vivid memories of what follows after Pooh has joined Rabbit. After a convivial "mouthful of something," Pooh tries to leave, gets stuck in Rabbit's door, where he remains for a week, comforted only by a Sustaining Book, until Christopher Robin and all Rabbit's friends-and-relations pull him out.

As a Wedged Bear in Great Tightness, Pooh is confined in a symbolic birth canal, while his emergence into freedom is the symbolic rebirth experienced by every participant in the Mysteries. We may wonder why Pooh needed the assistance not only of Christopher Robin but of all Rabbit's friends-and-relations as well. The answer is that he was warning his companions— and us—that progress in the Mysteries normally requires help. Those who attempt the journey alone run grave risks to mind and body alike.

Normally, the candidate should be guided by an

adept of superior expertise. By definition, this was impossible in the case of Pooh, himself the supreme adept. Doubtless the Sustaining Book would have supplied some of Christopher Robin's deficiencies. Tantalizingly, Milne does not identify it.

By now we have seen a symbolic descent into the Underworld and a symbolic rebirth. Having thus set up these two great symbols of initiation at the beginning of his work, Milne proceeds to show the steps by which Pooh brought his friends as far along the Way as their innate limitations allowed.

Piglet's Progress

The first thing Milne tells us about Piglet is that he "lived in a very grand house" (Chapter Three of *Winnie-the-Pooh*). Milne continues immediately,

> *One fine winter's day when Piglet was brushing away the snow in front of his house, he happened to look up, and there was Winnie-the-Pooh. Pooh was walking round and round in a circle, thinking of something else, and when Piglet called to him, he just went on walking.*

When Piglet asked what he was doing, " 'Tracking something,' said Winnie-the-Pooh very mysteriously."

It is yet another astonishing example of the blindness of generations of readers that—to the best of my
knowledge—no one has yet noted the cluster of initiatory references in just these two pages.

We cannot help noticing the powerful emphasis on
winter and snow that text and picture combine to give
us. Symbolically, of course, these strongly suggest the
north. Now, in many ceremonies of initiation, the candidate enters at the northern part of the place of initiation. Next we notice that Pooh is walking in a circle.
The circle has many esoteric meanings. It is a world-
wide symbol of eternity, and we are all familiar with
"the magic circle." Here, though, it refers to the candidate's progress during nearly all ceremonies of initiation. Whether or not this progress is literally circular, it
always goes round the cave, temple or other dedicated
place. It is also highly significant that Piglet has to ad-
dress Pooh twice before he answers. From what follows, it is clear that Pooh is testing Piglet. Those who
enter the Great Mysteries must show some interest and
aptitude before they are seriously considered as candidates. Milne does not tell us precisely what Piglet's first
words to Pooh were. He merely says that Piglet called
to him; presumably just a greeting. That was not
enough. It is only when Piglet asks, "What are you doing?" that Pooh answers.

His answer fully confirms our interpretation.

"Tracking something," he says, and he says it "very mysteriously." However the Ancient Mysteries differ in time, place and detail, all alike are tracking something, searching for something. It may be some lost wisdom, or spiritual perfection, self-knowledge or knowledge of another world. Milne's choice of the word "mysteriously" just at this point leaves us no excuse for misunderstanding.

A few lines later, we read a statement equally relevant and profound. When Piglet wonders what Pooh is tracking, Pooh answers, "I shall have to wait until I catch up with it." Like all the great mystics, Pooh proclaims that ultimate truth cannot be captured in words; it must be personally experienced.

Pooh draws Piglet's attention to the elusive nature of their quarry: "It may be [a Woozle] . . . Sometimes it is, and sometimes it isn't. You never can tell with pawmarks." He also points out the mysterious multiplication of footprints. More important are other pieces of evidence on the following pages.

Shepard's picture makes it clear that Pooh Bear and Piglet are walking round the spinney in a clockwise direction, that is, with the sun, following the traditions of all the Ancient Mysteries. Equally in accordance with tradition is Pooh's question: "Would you mind coming with me, Piglet, in case they [the Woozles or Wizzles] turn out to be Hostile Animals?"

In every Ancient Mystery, candidates had to prove their courage and determination by passing through some ordeal. Facing the unknown and possibly hostile Woozle—or Wizzle—was Piglet's first ordeal. And he passed it triumphantly, scratching "his ear in a nice sort of way" and saying "he would be delighted to come, in case it really *was* a Woozle."

It is true that his nerve is strained almost to the breaking point as the mysterious footprints multiply, but relief comes just in time, allowing him to retire without loss of face. At this stage, his courage is somewhat variable, and it oscillates frequently until he rises, as we know, to heroic heights at the end of the saga.

The conclusion of this chapter needs some comment, as it has often been wildly misunderstood. All too many readers have accepted Christopher Robin's commonplace and materialistic explanation of the multiplying footsteps. As we reported in the previous chapter, he believed that the footsteps had been made, first by Pooh alone, and then by Pooh and Piglet together; and that the apparent multiplication had been caused by the fact that they did not put their feet in exactly the same places on each circuit.

Armed with the knowledge we have all acquired, we can see that this is a matter of the difference between exoteric and esoteric knowledge. Esoteric knowledge is for the initiate and for the initiate only. Exoteric knowledge suffices the superficial and materialistic, such as Christopher Robin. Plausible, even eminently rational though it is, it hides the deeper truth.

Pooh's apparent agreement with Christopher Robin signals his reluctant recognition of that amiable boy's limitations. The delusion with which he reproaches himself was his too hopeful belief that Christopher Robin was capable of the Great Mysteries.

Even at this stage, the kindly Bear can rekindle hope. Christopher Robin says, " 'You're the Best Bear in All the World.' 'Am I?' said Pooh hopefully." Clearly his hope was that Christopher Robin's words indicated a true appreciation of the Enormous Brain, and consequently a chance that he might learn from it. Alas! We must feel that, on this occasion, Pooh's benevolence outweighed his judgment.

As we remarked earlier, Piglet's mind is still liable to violent oscillations. Nowhere is this more evident than "In Which Piglet Meets a Heffalump." To repeat the account of events so recently outlined would be tedious, but some comments are necessary. The chapter opens with Christopher Robin's statement that he had seen a Heffalump that day. After the extraordinarily vague conversation we have already analyzed, Pooh and Piglet walk home together. Almost silent at first, "they began to talk in a friendly way about this and that . . . And then, just as they came to the Six Pine Trees, Pooh looked round to see that nobody was listening, and said in a very solemn voice: 'Piglet, I have decided something.' "

We cannot doubt that the decision is one of major importance. It has been carefully prepared and the scene has been set with meticulous care. Though Milne chose not to reveal the exact subject Piglet and Pooh were discussing, the scraps of conversation he did report strongly suggest serious thought rather than trivial chatter:

Piglet said, "If you see what I mean, Pooh," and Pooh said, "It's just what I think myself, Piglet." Obviously Piglet had volunteered a statement which had earned the reward of his guru's agreement. Emboldened by this, Piglet ventures the apparently independent " 'But, on the other hand, Pooh, we must remember,' and Pooh said, 'Quite true, Piglet, although I had forgotten it for the moment.' "

We must pause briefly to question the meaning of Pooh's statement that he had forgotten for the moment. We cannot take it literally, of course. Real forgetfulness is incompatible with Satori or Perfect Enlightenment. It would totally undermine Pooh's credibility as Supreme Magus of the Second Millennium. What then must we think?

Two explanations come readily to mind. Pooh's

pretense of forgetfulness might simply be an innocent ruse to imbue the still somewhat timid Piglet to greater self-confidence by reducing the too awe-inspiring distance between him and his master. Or "moment" might here have its ancient meaning of "great importance," and Pooh might be saying that he had relegated the topic of their conversation to the back of his mind— "forgotten" it in that sense only—for the *sake* of the moment—that is, for the sake of the momentous initiatory ordeal to which he was now leading Piglet. The moment seemed propitious. Piglet seemed to show precisely that mixture of trustful deference and boldness needed for the next step on the Way of the Initiate. The place too was carefully chosen. They had come to the Six Pine Trees.

Both species and number are profoundly significant. In Brehon (Ancient Irish) law, the pine was a tree of the highest rank: one of the Chieftain Trees; "the courtly pine" an ancient Welsh poem calls it. In an esoteric context, we cannot see the number six without thinking of the hexagram, that six-pointed figure also known as the Star of David and the Seal of Solomon, and formed by two interlocked triangles. Let us also remember that, among other things, it indicates the creative union of the female and male principles, and the four elements that were the building blocks of ancient physics. Even more esoterically, by adding the number four of the elements to the three of either triangle, we get the mystic number seven. This does not appear on the hexagram but it was supposed to be there invisibly and to emerge to the inner eye of the true Magus who meditated on this symbol.

No wonder that "Pooh looked round to see that nobody else was listening." No wonder either that he spoke "in a very solemn voice."

Readers who know the incident of the Heffalump, and have followed this chapter so far, may be wondering how it will continue. How, they may be thinking, can I possibly defend Winnie-ther-Pooh as Piglet's guru when the story begins with a blatantly impracticable Heffalump Trap and ends with Piglet in bed with a headache and Pooh with his head stuck in a honey jar? Whether we regard the Heffalump as an imaginary being or—quite impossibly—as a misnomer for an elephant, surely the whole thing was not only a total failure but a farcical failure, leaving both stripped of their dignity.

I ask such readers to think again, even to read

again. What are the last four sentences of the Heffalump chapter?

*But Christopher Robin and Pooh went home to
breakfast together.*

*"Oh, Bear!" said Christopher Robin. "How I do
love you!"*

"So do I," said Pooh.

Let us concentrate on Pooh's obvious satisfaction
with the final situation of the Heffalump quest. How
could this be?

We can easily dismiss his undignified position with
his head stuck in the empty jar of honey. Only those
whose dignity is superficial are afraid of losing it. Those
familiar with the surprising methods of some Zen masters will remember parallels. The truly important matter here is Piglet's state of mind.

We have already seen him in bed with a headache,
but that same sentence tells us "Then Piglet saw what a
Foolish Piglet he had been." In other words, he had
made a valuable advance in self-knowledge. Now, this is
often a painful experience, but it is essential for every
pilgrim on the Way of the Mysteries. And the Way itself
is fraught with perils. Only courage and determination
can overcome them.

Never again, we may be sure, will Piglet fail the

test, as he did when he took Pooh's absurd plan for catching a Heffalump at its face value. Surely such a vast step forward is worth a headache. Anyway, his suffering was apparently neither long nor disabling. Nor was Pooh neglecting him. When we meet them next, "Outside his [Pooh's] house he found Piglet, jumping up and down trying to reach the knocker." When Piglet explains what he was trying to do, note the exquisite tact with which Pooh restores Piglet's confidence, perhaps shaken by the Heffalump incident: " 'Let me do it for you,' said Pooh kindly. So he reached up and knocked at the door." After digressing to tell Piglet about Eeyore's sadness because no one has remembered his birthday, Pooh continues,

"What a long time whoever lives here is answering this door." And he knocked again.

"But Pooh," said Piglet, "it's your own house!"

"Oh!" said Pooh. "So it is," he said. "Well, let's go in."

Immediately we notice Piglet's improved perceptiveness and confidence. Whereas at the beginning of the Heffalump incident, he had blindly accepted an unreal situation and failed to challenge Pooh's deliberately absurd suggestion, now he recognizes reality and boldly points out the absurdity of Pooh's knocking at his own door. Surely this must dispel any doubt concerning the deep wisdom of Pooh's guidance in the previous episode.

Pooh himself records his satisfaction, first by his quiet "So it is," then by inviting Piglet into the house. In this situation, even the most casual can hardly miss the symbolic significance of the sequence: Piglet tries to knock on the door but the knocker is, as the illustration confirms, out of his reach; then Pooh knocks for him; finally, Pooh takes Piglet into his house, the house of wisdom. Could anything be clearer and more complete?

Piglet's part in giving Eeyore a birthday present does not need analysis in this context except to remind us of his continued special association with Pooh. Similarly, his taking Roo's place in Kanga's pouch will be more fitly considered in Chapter Ten. When my readers think back to Pooh's ingenuity and heroism during the flood, they will now understand it was no mere chance that it was Piglet he rescued. So far, however, we have not considered one important element in this situation.

When we read of Piglet in "the Terrible Flood" we think immediately of the Biblical Great Flood, and so inevitably of Noah and the Ark. At first, the analogy may seem rather remote. Given the literary conventions of the genre in which Milne was working, we have no difficulty in accepting one "Very Small Animal" as the representative of all living creatures. Can we, though, accept Christopher Robin's inverted umbrella as an adequate symbol of the Ark?

Reduction of scale is no problem, but what about shape? *The Brain of Pooh* is circular: The Ark was fundamentally rectangular. How can we reconcile this apparent contradiction? On closer consideration, we see that what at first seems an objection is in fact powerful evidence in our favor. In the previous chapter, we reminded ourselves of Eliphas Levi's dictum that squaring the circle was a characteristic power of the true Magus. This enabled us to accept Christopher Robin's oblong table as a satisfactory symbol of Arthur's Round Table. Equally, we can accept the round *Brain of Pooh* as a satisfactory symbol of Noah's Ark. Indeed, the substitution of round for oblong perfectly balances the substitution of oblong for round, and so supplies an elegant proof of the correctness of our interpretation.

If any further confirmation is needed, it stares us in the face when we look at the very name "Winnie." The letter *n,* here emphasized by doubling, is equivalent to the Hebrew letter "nun," the initial of Noah! "Nun" is also associated with the zodiacal sign of Pisces, the water element. We cannot complain that our author failed to give us guidance.

When A. A. Milne returned to his great theme after the two-year gap (1926–1928), he was careful to emphasize the special connection between Winnie-the-Pooh and Piglet in the first chapter of *The House At Pooh Corner.* Its opening words are, "One day when Pooh Bear had nothing else to do, he thought he would do something, so he went round to Piglet's house to see what Piglet was doing."

Finding that Piglet is out, Pooh returns home to discover Piglet waiting for him there. After "a little smackerel of something," they go off together to sing Pooh's latest hum to Eeyore. Snow is falling steadily, and "in a little while Piglet was wearing a white muffler round his neck and feeling more snowy behind the ears than he had ever felt before." Though clearly uncomfortable, "he didn't want Pooh to think he was Giving In," so he perseveres.

His growing strength of character is paralleled by his intellectual development. In the past, he had often been excessively suggestible, and inclined to take literally statements that were obvious jokes or fantasies. When Pooh has sung of his toes growing cold, "after thinking the matter out carefully . . . 'Pooh,' he [Piglet] said solemnly, 'it isn't the *toes* so much as the *ears*.'"

Here we see Piglet thinking for himself, using his own experience, and even venturing—apparently, at least—to contradict the Great Bear. In fact, of course, he is not really contradicting Pooh but simply reporting a different experience. Even this took considerable moral courage. No wonder he had to think carefully and that he spoke solemnly. Pooh Bear signals his recognition of Piglet's progress, first by singing his new song with Piglet another six times, thus making the mystic total of seven. An even more impressive accolade follows.

All Ursinologists will remember that Pooh and Piglet then proceed to build a house for Eeyore. As an example of practical benevolence, this is obvious enough. I fear, however, that its Pythagorean and Hermetic significances have been generally overlooked. As long ago as the fifth century B.C., the Pythagoreans had taught that the world had a mathematical basis. Platonists and, even more, Neo-Platonists, developed it into a theory that the secret of earthly beauty lay in discovering the mathematical proportions on which the universe was built and applying them to the arts, most especially to architecture. This, of course, was an obvious example of the Hermetic maxim "As above, so it is below."

Pooh alerts us to the mathematical form of Eeyore's house when he tells Piglet, "We will build it here . . . just by this wood, out of the wind, because this is where I thought of it. And we will call this Pooh Corner. And we will build an Eeyore House with sticks at Pooh Corner for Eeyore."

He adds, ". . . I could call this place Poohanpiglet Corner if Pooh Corner didn't sound better, which it does, being smaller and more like a corner."

Note the word "corner" five times in as many lines, and four times capitalized. There could hardly be a clearer signpost. Shepard's picture of the completed house is more than ample confirmation. The ground plan is clearly rectangular, the elevation as clearly triangular.

When Eeyore finds his new house, he thinks it is the one he built himself and that the wind has simply moved it to a new position. It is pleasing to record that, despite this laughable mistake, Eeyore does appreciate

the improvement, commenting, "Here it is as good as ever. In fact, better in places."

This initiation of Piglet into Pythagorean mystical mathematics and Hermeticism follows naturally on Pooh's leading Piglet through the door to wisdom. From now on, Piglet's progress to his apotheosis as Winnie-ther-Pooh's chosen companion is too self-evident to need any further explanation. Let us now look at the more limited but still real progress of Pooh's other friends.

The Progress of Pooh's Other Friends

Christopher Robin. We have already seen that the reference to Christopher Robin in his bath—at the very beginning of the Pooh cycle—implies that his was not the Way of the Magus. All that Pooh's benign influence could do was to make him the best kind of earthbound humanity, a twentieth-century equivalent of King Arthur. Any hopes of a loftier destiny were nullified when we read, "One fine day Pooh had stumped up to the top of the Forest to see if his friend Christopher Robin was interested in Bears at all." Far from being interested in Bears—note the significant capital *B* implying Bear as Master of occult wisdom—Christopher Robin was engrossed in plans for his Expotition to the North Pole, which displayed both his competence as a leader and his blindness to the deeper significance of the Quest.

Rabbit seems too deeply enmeshed in daily trivialities to advance beyond the rank of doorkeeper to the Mysteries, where we find him in Chapter Two. This too, however, is an essential though humble role. Nor should we undervalue the tribute in the Hum of Pooh which goes:

> *And a Help-yourself with Rabbit*
> *Though it may become a habit,*
> *Is a* pleasant *sort of habit*
> *For a Pooh.*

Moreover, Rabbit does toward the end of the opus show an increasing capacity for learning. Usually somewhat impatient, Rabbit is the one who proclaims the lesson of patience to the other players of Poohsticks: "They always take longer than you think." Finally, he shows a surprising advance in humility when, after the disastrous failure of his plan to unbounce Tigger, he recognizes "just the beautiful way a Tigger ought to bounce," and greets him with a heartfelt, "Oh, Tigger, I *am* glad to see you."

Eeyore too makes considerable progress. Right at the beginning, we saw his enquiring interest in the deepest questions of philosophical thought. His difficulties were emotional and moral rather than intellectual. Too much of a solitary Diogenes for most of the book, he does increasingly join in the activities of the other Forest-dwellers. It is a marked advance in amiability that he so quickly overcomes his first indignation when Tigger boffs him into the river and they go off happily together. Finally he accepts Rabbit's advice to go and see his friends. " 'There may be something in what you say, Rabbit,' he said at last. '. . . I must move about more. I must come and go.' " And so we find him taking a leading part in Proposing a Rissolution and reading his own poem to Christopher Robin in the last chapter.

How he will develop from here it would be presumptuous to predict. We can say, though, that several paths now lie open to him.

Two other characters are far too important to be dismissed in a paragraph or two. Owl will receive special attention in the next chapter, and Kanga in Chapter Ten.

9

POOH AND THE
QABALAH

By this stage of our studies, it would be superfluous to labor the obvious fact that the tree that Pooh climbs in search of honey is, Qabalistically speaking, the Sephirotic Tree, of which there is more later. As always, we can be confident that profound wisdom inspired our author in placing this incident at the very beginning of his incomparable guide to the Ancient Mysteries. No less an authority than Dr. Robert Wang reminds us that the Qabalah is basic to all Western occultism. Readers may wonder then why it did not come first in our little guide. For this there are three good reasons. (Note that mystical number. These things are not accidental, least of all when we are dealing with the Qabalah.)

First, the very depth and breadth of the subject make it exceptionally difficult for the beginner. As we shall show later, Christopher Robin's total incomprehension demonstrates this with painful clarity. Doubt-less Milne's account of this was intended to warn us that the Qabalah must be approached with patience and ef-fort. The more expert readers will, I am confident, un-derstand the difficulty, and be patient with those still on the lower rungs of the mystical ladder. They may even have enjoyed a quiet smile to themselves as they recog-nized the inner meaning of Qabalistic references in ear-lier chapters of this book. Such silent recognitions and sapient smiles are indeed among the rewards of our progress along the Mystic Way.

Second, prepared by their progress through the earlier chapters, all earnest seekers after truth will now be ready for at least the most elementary stage of Qa-balistic knowledge, and thereby achieve a deeper un-derstanding of what has gone before. They will see clearly the profound unity that underlies all the Ancient Mysteries. They will realize that the Great Bear has not been guiding us through fascinating but unrelated worlds of mystery but showing us that, as Alexander Pope said, "all are but parts of one stupendous whole."

Third, without at least an elementary grasp of the Qabalah, the reader would hardly be able to accept the astonishing revelation in Chapter Ten that crowns our Ursinian studies of mystical truth and initiates us into our task as guides to the new Millennium.

What Is the Qabalah?

Qabalah—also variously spelled "Cabala," "Cabbala," "Kabala" and so on—is an ancient Hebrew tradition giving a hidden meaning to the Hebrew Scriptures, a meaning revealed only to the initiates. Some Qabalists claimed the secret had originally been communicated to Adam by an angel, and then handed down orally for many generations. The two major Qabalistic works, the *Sepher Yetzirah* and the *Zohar,* were first printed in the sixteenth century, though there were older manuscript editions.

Qabalists represented the universe in the form of a diagram known as the Sephirotic Tree of Life (see opposite). Above the Tree are three beings of unimaginable abstraction, the three Veils, named, in ascending order, Ain Soph Aur, Ain Soph and Ain. These transmit the creative power from its even more incomprehensible source above to the ten Sephiroth on the Tree. Different Qabalists describe the Sephiroth in various ways, but their names give us some indication, and we can say with confidence that Winnie-ther-Pooh's ascent and descent of the honey tree symbolize his rise to the heights (Kether, the Crown) and his return to earth (Malkuth) in order to spread his benign influence there.

Because Milne has given so many symbolic meanings to this tree, its Qabalistic significance might be

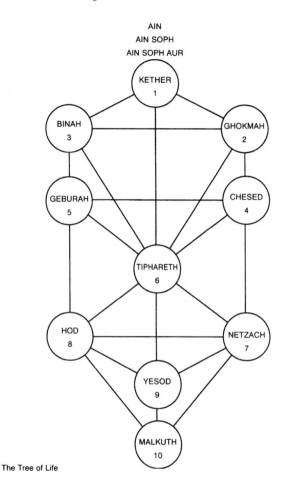

The Tree of Life

missed, but no Qabalistically trained Ursinologist could fail to see our author's meaning when he wrote in the "Contradiction" to *The House At Pooh Corner:*

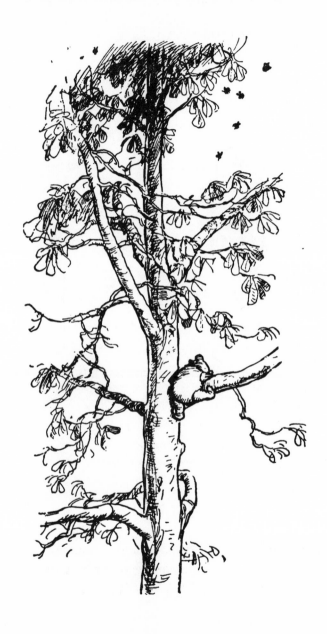

Pooh, sitting wakeful a little longer on his chair by our pillow, thinks Grand Thoughts to himself about Nothing, until he, too, closes his eyes and nods his head, and follows us on tiptoe into the Forest.

"Grand Thoughts to himself about Nothing": The phrase clearly signals that Pooh, staying awake after the others were all asleep, concentrates his Enormous Brain on the supreme mystery of the Qabalah. The essential quality of the three Veils was that they were Pure Being and therefore Nothing.

This may appear paradoxical but the basic idea is simple enough. When we imagine any particular being we know, it inevitably has a shape, and a shape involves limits. Pure, Limitless Being therefore has no shape. So we cannot picture it or even define it, for defining literally means limiting. So Pure Being is No Thing, Nothing. Nothing, but the No Thing from which all things emanate. Now we can see why Pooh needed solitude

and silence to contemplate this unimaginable mystery.

We understand too why he closes his eyes before he joins his companions in the Forest. For the life of the Forest, rich and joyous though it is, with all its "magic adventures," is a mere dream compared with that ultimate reality that the Great Bear alone can approach, though even he cannot experience it.

This, incidentally, explains a passage that may have puzzled some readers as they studied an early section of the Expotition to the North Pole. Though that chapter primarily concerned the esoteric meanings of Arthurian tales, it is not surprising to find Qabalistic references as well. When Pooh is probing Christopher Robin's understanding of the Quest, he asks him,

> *"Where are we going to on this Expotition?"*
> *"Expedition, silly old Bear. It's got an 'x' in it."*
> *"Oh!" said Pooh. "I know." But he didn't really.*

Why, many readers have asked, bring an x to show the difference between "Expedition" and "Expotition," when x is equally present in both? Again, how, in this particular context, should we interpret the statement "But he [Pooh] didn't really [know what *Expedition* meant]"?

The first question is easy enough to answer. As x is the most widely used symbol for an unknown quantity, it is signalling the presence of an unknown, obviously an important unknown. In our Qabalistic context, this powerfully suggests the unknown, indeed unknowable, Ain. But also, x equals ten in Roman numerals; and ten, of course, is the number of Malkuth—the earth—on the Sephirotic Tree. Thus, once again, by an astonishing yet typical paradox, Pooh combines the most exalted spirituality with a firm grasp of everyday reality.

Now we turn to the second question. At first, we might be tempted to dismiss Pooh's ignorance as just another example of that mask which Pooh so often wore. But this is far too glib. It entirely neglects the source of the statement: not one of the uninitiated outsiders, not Pooh disguising his true powers. No: This comes from our author himself. What, then, does it mean?

With the author's words fresh in our memories, the answer, in Qabalistic terms, is clear. In this context, the goal of the quest is ultimate truth, ultimate reality; in other words, Ain. And Pooh alone is aware that this is unattainable. Milne makes this abundantly clear when he says, "He didn't really." The "really" tells us that Pooh's inability to know the unknowable was a realistic recognition that such knowledge was impossible.

Now we turn to an area where Qabalistic knowledge is not only possible but, at least in its elementary stages, simple. I refer to *gematria*.

Gematria

Gematria (Qabalistic numerology) is based on the fact that each of the twenty-two letters of the Hebrew alphabet is also a number. Qabalists applied this to the interpretation of the Scriptures by translating words into numbers and discovering hidden relations and meanings by finding other words in the Bible whose letters added up to the same total. To take an example from our own text: In the previous chapter, I mentioned that Winnie-the-Pooh functioned in a Noah-like capacity when he rescued Piglet from the flood. Let us see whether *gematria* supports this identification. If we transliterate "Pooh" into the Hebrew alphabet, we get Heh, Oin, Oin, Peh. I am, of course, following the Hebrew rule, writing from right to left. Now let us assign the accepted numbers to those letters, again reading them from right to left. The result is $5 + 70 + 70 + 80 = 225$. Following the same process with Noah, we get Heh, Aleph, Oin, Nun. Substituting the numbers, we get $5 + 1 + 70 + 50 = 126$.

At first sight, 225 and 126 hardly shout an obvious answer. But the resources of *gematria* are far from exhausted. Adding the digits from both totals—$2 + 2 + 5$ and $1 + 2 + 6$—what do we get? Nine in both cases! Could we ask for better Qabalistic proof that Pooh in this instance is equivalent to Noah?

We may now look back at the "Contradiction." Perhaps nothing is more deplorable to the true Ursinian scholar than the widespread neglect of Milne's introductory passages. We can understand, and even sympathize with, the readers' desire to hurry on to the fascinating narratives which follow, but these cannot be properly understood without the careful preparation Milne provided for us.

This is strikingly clear at the beginning of paragraph two of the Contradiction.

Christopher Robin said to me, "What about that story you were going to tell me about what happened to Pooh when—" I happened to say very quickly, "What about nine times a hundred and seven?"

Could we possibly have a clearer statement of that basic Qabalistic principle that a sound understanding of *gematria* must precede any deep reading of a text? Thus admonished, let us look at the examples before us.

Even without any manipulation, these numbers are strikingly significant. We have already demonstrated that 9 is the number of Pooh himself; that 1 is the monad that created the world, nought or 0 the shapeless No Thing out of which the world was formed, and 7 the traditional period of creation in Mosaic cosmogony. So we can see right away that multiplying 9 (Pooh) by

107 (the universe) underlines the universal power and knowledge of the Great Bear. Of course, there is far more to it than that.

Nine times 107 equals 963: 9, 6, 3. We have already come across the Sephirotic Tree, with Kether, the Crown, at the top, and Malkuth, the Kingdom, at the bottom. Each of these Sephiroth is numbered. Between Kether (1) and Malkuth (10) are the other Sephiroth, numbered 2 to 9. Applying the three numbers we have discovered, we find 9 is Yesod, the Foundation; 6 is Tiphareth, Beauty or the Sun; 3 is Binah, Understanding or the Queen. What could be plainer or more convincingly descriptive of the Milnean text? A sound Foundation supporting Beauty and Understanding. Note also the alternative meanings for Tiphareth and Binah: the Sun and the Queen. One gives additional confirmation to what we have pointed out in earlier chapters about solar influences; the other will be explained in the next chapter.

Naturally, Milne did not leave it at that. He went on to pose the problem "about cows going through a gate at two a minute, and there are three hundred in the field, so how many are left after an hour and a half?" I fear there have been some readers who did not work out this simple sum and so did not see its esoteric meaning. It goes thus:

The number remaining in the field is the original

300 minus the number that left. At 2 cows leaving per minute for 90 minutes, 180 will have left after an hour and a half. Therefore the number remaining in the field is 300 minus 180, which is 120.

The number 120 may be separated into 12 and 0. Twelve is the number of the Signs of the Zodiac, a symbol of the material, manifest world. Zero is the number of the unmanifest, that is, Ain. So here we have a plain signpost to the world of the Qabalah.

If we needed anything more to realize the importance of this passage, Milne supplies it in the very next sentence after the mathematical problems: "We find these very exciting." I fear that all too many readers have taken this as a casual joke. We should all remember that an essential qualification for all who would practice hermeneutics (the systematic study of interpretation) is the intuitive ability to distinguish passages that need elaborate decoding from those that should be accepted at their face value.

In this case, when Milne tells us that these problems are very exciting, so exciting indeed that "when we have been excited quite enough, we curl up and go to sleep," we should take him quite literally, since the problems lead us into the passage which told of Pooh's contemplation of Pure Being. Our author placed his initials at the end of this passage, and we can now see that this did much more than authenticate it: it gave yet another clear reference to the Sephirotic Tree. Transliterating A.A.M. into Hebrew, we get Mem, Aleph, Aleph, numerically equivalent to 40 + 1 + 1, which adds up to 42. And this is the total of the 10 Sephiroth plus the 32 Paths of Wisdom!

Adam Kadmon

Incidentally, a development of the Sephirotic Tree explains a passage that has worried some true Ursinologists and even seemed to give ammunition to those who derided all claims for Pooh's intellectual greatness. I am referring to an incident in the chapter where Rabbit's attempt to unbounce Tigger leads to his losing his friends in the fog. They are discussing which direction to take.

> *"I think it's more to the right," said Piglet nervously. "What do you think, Pooh?"*
>
> *Pooh looked at his two paws. He knew that one of them was the right, and he knew that when you had decided which one of them was the right, then the other one was the left, but he never could remember how to begin.*

Can we really, the mockers say, take seriously the wisdom of a person who can't even tell his left paw from his right? No doubt many of my readers will have clear and convincing answers to this objection, but here I should like to supply the Qabalistic answer.

As well as the Sephirotic Tree, Qabalists also used the image of the Archetypal Man, Adam Kadmon, who existed before the earthly Adam. (We should note in passing that "Man" is misleading, as Adam Kadmon contained both female and male potency.) The ten Sephiroth were distributed over the body of Adam Kadmon, just as they were on the tree. One side corresponded to the Pillar of Severity, the other to the Pillar of Mercy, with the Pillar of Mildness in the middle. So when Pooh was looking at his paws, he was, as a symbol of Adam Kadmon, contemplating the Sephiroth and considering which was more relevant to the situation. The possible objection that "he never could remember how to begin" falls to the ground when we recollect how long and intimate his relationship with the Sephiroth was. Memory, in any ordinary use of the word, had long ago been transformed into habit; in this case, the habit of judging intuitively whether severity or mildness was called for.

Obviously I could continue at length with examples of Pooh Bear's profound mastery of Qabalah, but I feel that this is the chapter which should specially celebrate the learning and particularly the verbal dexterity of Owl. Whereas Pooh's Qabalism is but one aspect of his multifaceted genius, Owl's essentially scholarly approach makes him peculiarly fit to represent Qabalism in this book.

Owl as a Qabalistic Scholar

Milne presents Owl as the archetypal scholar. One can easily picture him as an Oxford or Cambridge don of the old school. Precise and polysyllabic in speech. A lover of anecdote; though, alas, we never hear the whole of the story he was telling Christopher Robin "about an accident which had nearly happened to a friend of his whom Christopher Robin didn't know," or the story about what happened to his uncle Robert on a blusterous day.

His lifestyle was equally typical. When his furniture was being removed after the disaster to his house,

Kanga said, " 'You won't want this dirty old dish-cloth any more, will you, and what about this carpet, it's all in holes,' and Owl was calling back indignantly, 'Of course I do! It's just a question of arranging the furniture properly, and it isn't a dish-cloth, it's my shawl.' "

Owl clearly exhibited that indifference to domestic niceties often characteristic of the unworldly scholar.

On the other hand, all the Forest-dwellers recognize his learning. Owl "Knows Things," said Piglet to himself. Our author tells us that "Owl [was] wise in many ways." His ability to spell Tuesday irresistibly commands respect. Most impressive of all is the tribute of the Great Bear himself:

"And if anyone knows anything about anything," *said Bear to himself, "it's Owl who knows something* *about something," he said, "or my name's not Winnie-* *the-Pooh," he said. "Which it is," he added. "So there* *you are."*

What more convincing testimonial could we have than this emphatic statement, explicitly underwritten by the Great Name?

So far, however, though we have established Owl's credentials as a great scholar in general, we have still to show he is a great Qabalistic scholar. The author alerts our Qabalistic attention when we first meet Owl. You

will remember that Pooh sought him out at the very beginning of his search for Eeyore's tail. When he arrives
at Owl's door, he studies its two notices: "PLES RING
IF AN RNSER IS REQIRD" and "PLEZ CNOKE IF
AN RNSR IS NOT REQID."

Winnie-the-Pooh read the two notices very carefully, first from left to right, and afterward, in case he
had missed some of it, from right to left.

Perceptive readers will have picked up the message of the last twelve words. Why should he read from
right to left? What might he have missed by reading
only from left to right? What relevant language must be
read from right to left? Hebrew, of course, the language
of the Qabalah!

This, I think, is the proper place to answer a question that I suspect may be troubling some of my
readers. Have I not been suppressing vital evidence, evidence that weakens if it does not destroy Owl's claim to
learning? When I proclaimed his ability to spell Tuesday, I failed to add that he spelled it wrong. When
I quoted the praise of Owl's wisdom, I failed to add
that he "went all to pieces over delicate words like
MEASLES and BUTTERED TOAST."

Anyone who has followed me this far must feel
deeply puzzled. We all know enough by now to dismiss
as obviously ridiculous the notion that Owl simply could
not spell these words. So what does this passage mean?

As always, the text gives the clues, if we look carefully enough. Here the key phrase is "delicate words." Why are MEASLES and BUTTERED TOAST delicate words? This answer inevitably lies in *gematria*.

Before I apply this, I must explain that the Hebrew alphabet does not contain the vowel *e*. This must be supplied by the context or the informed intuition of the interpreter. Transliterating the English letters into Hebrew and then giving the latter their numerical equivalents, we reach the following:

MEASLES comes out as Samech (60), Lamed (30), Samech (60), Aleph (1), Mem (40). These numbers add up to 191. The digits, 1, 9, 1, total 11. Now in one major system of numerology, 11 is the evil number, the number of defeat and death. Dismissing this as obviously inappropriate, we proceed to the next step, and add our two digits: 1 + 1 and get 2. Two, the dyad! The numerical representative of Yin and Yang, the male and female principles: the major secret, which we are only now approaching.

BUTTERED TOAST is even more complex, that is, more "delicate" in Milne's own phrase. Applying the standard methods, we find that BUTTERED gives us Daleth (4), Resh (200), Tau (400), Tau (400), Vau (6), Beth (2): total 1012, whose digits add up to 4. TOAST gives us Tau (400), Samech (60), Aleph (1), Oin (70), Tau (400): total 931, whose digits add up to 13.

Innumerable interpretations leap off the page at us. Most obviously, 4 is the number of weeks in a lunar month, and there are 13 lunar months in a year. So the annual cycle of lunar influences is there, influences especially natural to Owl, an archetypical creature of the night. The number 4 appears twice; first overtly, then as the 1 plus 3 of 13. Four, of course, represents the square of the universe and the 4 elements that composed it in ancient science. Add 4 to 13. The resulting 17 contains both 1, the monad that created the universe, and 7, the number of the days of creation in Hebrew cosmogony. Take the butter off the toast, that is, deduct 4 from 13, and we are back to 9, the number of Pooh himself! These are merely the first interpretations that I saw at a quick and casual inspection. Even these, however, fully justify the claim that the Qabalah is both the foundation and the summing up of all esoteric wisdom.

Now we understand why MEASLES and BUTTERED TOAST were delicate words. Again, we can now see what Milne meant when he said Owl "went all to pieces" over them. Going all to pieces is an arcane way of saying that he analyzed all the components of these words, and may well have decided they and their interpretations should be reserved for the initiated, such as my readers.

In Chapter Five, Rabbit goes to ask Owl to explain two cryptic notices from Christopher Robin. Let us focus on one phrase in the second message, the phrase "Bisy Backson." We know this is the key phrase, because, as soon as Rabbit utters it—

> *Owl gave a great sigh of relief.*
> *"Ah!" said Owl. "Now we know where we are."*

Applying *gematria* and going through the usual process of transliterating "Bisy Backson" into Hebrew letters, finding the numerical equivalents and adding them up, we reach the total of 765. Now, 765 is the date when pictorial printing is first recorded in Japan. We also note that $7 + 6 + 5 = 18$; it was about 18 years earlier that the first printed newspaper appeared in Peking. What could be more striking than this Qabalistic link between printing in the Far East and Owl, who is uniquely connected with printed notices in the Pooh books, a connection Milne was at pains to bring to our attention! I think I may take a modest pride in pointing out that this demonstrates that the Qabalah, often applied only in Western occult tradition, can equally illuminate the remotest regions of Asia.

Qabalah Throws Light on the Tarot

Readers of our chapter on the tarot may remember that, while accepting Gershom Scholem's dismissal of any original connection of Qabalah with the tarot, I said that Qabalah might nevertheless help us to elucidate the Milnean references to the tarot. Such readers might legitimately expect some examples of this. Of the many possible instances, I select three: two, throwing further light on passages in Chapter Five; the other, illuminating an incident not so far mentioned in this book.

When talking of Eeyore as the tarot Fool, I reminded my readers that the number of the Fool was zero, and added that zero stood for the elemental nothingness out of which the universe was created. Unsupported, this statement might perhaps seem dogmatic and lacking in clarity. After the explanation of the Qabalistic doctrine of emanations from the creative Nothingness down through the Sephirotic Tree, there should be no further difficulty in understanding this passage.

Similarly, the rather surprising identification of Rabbit with the card of the Universe is confirmed by *gematria,* which gives the name of Rabbit a total of 615, whose digits add up to 12: the number of the signs of the zodiac, an obvious symbol of the world.

Now for a hitherto unexamined facet of the World of Pooh. Close students of this world have long pondered the curious relationship of Eeyore and Owl. At first sight, they could hardly appear more opposite. Owl is the Forest's outstanding representative of learning

and literacy; Eeyore—apart from his abortive experiment with the letter *A*—rejects both: " 'Education,' said
Eeyore bitterly, jumping on his six sticks. 'What *is* learning?' " Until the last winter, Eeyore lived alone, house-
less in "a thistly corner of the forest"; in sharp contrast,
"Owl lived at The Chestnuts, an old-world residence of
great charm, which was grander than anybody else's."

It is noticeable that Milne and Shepard both kept
these two apart. The only time they appear together in
Winnie-the-Pooh is near the end, at the party Christopher Robin gave for Pooh. Even here, they are clearly
ignoring each other. By the end of *The House At Pooh
Corner,* they have grown close. On page 163, when all
Christopher Robin's friends meet "to pass a Rissolution," the two are sitting next to each other. More strik-

ingly, in the very last picture to show the company together, Eeyore and Owl are flanking Pooh. What is the
answer to this enigma?

We find it precisely in Qabalistic tarot. Dr. Robert
Wang, the foremost authority on this subject, identifies
the Fool with his apparent opposite, the Hermit, for the
Hermit is "the wise old age of the Child" (or Fool). So
we now understand the long separation and final close-
ness of Eeyore and Owl. Milne and Shepard obviously
judged that to present two different ages of the same
character simultaneously might confuse their readers.
The mass of misunderstanding and misreading I have
met in my researches for this small and elementary
treatise on the occult aspects of the text proves all too
plainly that author and artist judged well.

As always, though, they gave a hint to the more

perceptive readers. The first incident involving Eeyore tells us that Pooh found Eeyore's missing tail serving as a bell-pull at Owl's house. This is also Owl's first appearance. The significance of the fact that both appear for the first time in relation to one another is obvious enough. By now, my readers will doubtless take it for granted that I have applied *gematria* to the notice regarding the bell-pull: "PLES RING IF AN RNSER IS REQIRD." I have, and—omitting the calculations, which those interested can now perform for themselves—the answer is six: the Sephira of Beauty. Beauty is the natural result of combining the questing youth of the Fool, here symbolized by Eeyore, and the experienced wisdom of the Hermit, here symbolized by Owl. Could any answer be more satisfying, both intellectually and aesthetically?

Scientific study of Pooh as a psychologist is outside our present scope, but it would be wrong not to comment on a link between him and the father of psychoanalysis in the apparently remote subject of *gematria.* As they were reading the examples of *gematria,* readers who are familiar with Freud's *Psychopathology of Everyday Life* must often have had a sense of *déjà vu.* Freud's section on "Determinism" in Chapter Twelve contains several pages on numbers. Here Freud argued that the unconscious mind determines apparently random choices of numbers, so that the numbers chosen always refer to something significant for the chooser. The arithmetical manipulations that Freud uses to produce significant results are remarkably similar to those of Qabalists using *gematria*. Inevitably, the question arises: was Freud a secret Qabalist?

Such a sensational suggestion demands far more attention than we can give it here. Leaving it—perhaps to the future—let us move to an aspect of Pooh, which is at least equally sensational but more relevant to our present study of the Ancient Mysteries.

10

POOH AND THE
FEMALE MYSTERIES

Now we arrive at the most astonishing revelation of all. In my opening chapter, I spoke of the great and unexpected discovery I had made in the course of my researches for this book: the discovery that the esoteric World of Pooh includes the ancient Female Mysteries. More than this, it is in connection with these that Winnie-ther-Pooh gives us perhaps his most important "missage" as Supreme Magus of the Second Millennium.

The most famous of the exclusively female Mysteries were the cult of the Bona Dea (the Good Goddess) in ancient Rome and the Thesmophoria in ancient Greece. The Thesmophoria developed into the Eleusinian Mysteries, which were open to males also; a clear allusion to the cooperation of Pooh and Kanga. Both Greek mysteries specially honored the Mother

Goddess, Demeter. We shall explore the implications of this later in the chapter.

My announcement in Chapter One may have surprised readers enough to alert them to relevant hints in the subsequent chapters. In the chapter on astrology, they may have noticed the occasional reversal of the usual assignment of masculinity to the sun and femininity to the moon. They may also have noticed the female elements in both the history and symbolism of alchemy; the many powerful female figures in the tarot, the equally powerful female influences in Arthurian legend, and the combination of male and female potencies in the Archetypal Adam Kadmon of the Qabalah.

Far more convincing, of course, than any words of a mere commentator are the words of the text itself. A key passage is placed at the very outset of our journey: "In Which We Are Introduced to Winnie-the-Pooh." Remembering that to be introduced meant "to be led into something," we know we are about to be conducted into some part of the mystery of the Great Bear. This passage, therefore, demands our closest attention. Christopher Robin has just brought Edward Bear down the stairs. Then—

Anyhow, here he is at the bottom, and ready to be introduced to you. Winnie-the-Pooh.

When I first heard his name, I said, just as you are going to say, "But I thought he was a boy?"

"So did I," said Christopher Robin.
"Then you can't call him Winnie?"
"I don't."
"But you said—"
"He's Winnie-ther-Pooh. Don't you know what 'ther' *means?"*

"Ah, yes, now I do," I said quickly; and I hope you do too, because it is all the explanation you are going to get.

Clearly *"ther"* is the key. Applying the method of *gematria* again, we find the dyad, the numerical symbol of Yin and Yang, the conjoined male and female principles! Now at last we begin to understand the full meaning of that hitherto puzzling name, with its profoundly androgynous implications. Note too that Christopher Robin's answers make it clear that he does not venture to *give* a name to the Great Bear: He merely recognizes that he is Winnie-ther-Pooh. A remarkable intuition for him.

So now we are led to the threshold, but it is left to us to cross that threshold by our own labors and enter into the temple itself. I must record my modest pride in being instrumental in the performance of those labors, showing the way to my Ursinian companions on the Path.

Some Objections

Even with this authoritative guidance from the text in front of us, some readers may still find difficulty in accepting the female element in the World of Pooh and especially in Pooh personally. They will point to the fact that Kanga is the only female in that world, and—worse still—that at first she appears as an intruder. A highly unwelcome intruder at that. Objectors will remind us that the first reaction of the original Forest-dwellers is to try to expel her and her offspring, Roo. As these objections are solidly based on the text itself, they cannot be lightly dismissed. We must examine them respectfully, while never forgetting the powerful counter-evidence.

Rabbit's Plan to Expel Kanga

Rabbit addresses Piglet and Pooh in characteristically "Captainish" style. He speaks of the arrival of this "Strange Animal," and goes on to propose that he and his friends should kidnap Baby Roo and make his return conditional on the permanent departure of these unwelcome newcomers. At first sight, this incident seems to convey an emphatically misogynistic message. Rabbit's principal objection to Kanga is that she is "an animal who carries her family about with her in her pocket!" We have already seen, on page 100, that Kanga's pouch was the nearest permissible reference to the womb. So Rabbit's objection was basically to her femaleness. He does also object to her as a newcomer, but we may suspect that this was an attempt to cloak his real objection to her as a female, a typical ploy of misogynists who know that open avowal of their prejudices has become socially unacceptable.

So far, so bad for our thesis. But wait and see what happens.

The plan succeeds to the extent that Rabbit does manage to carry off Roo and Piglet takes Roo's place in Kanga's pouch. But what happens when Kanga gets home and discovers the substitution?

Just for a moment, she thought she was frightened, and then she knew she wasn't; for she felt sure that Christopher Robin would never let any harm happen to Roo. So she said to herself, "If they are having a joke with me, I will have a joke with them."

Pretending that she does not notice the substitution, she gives the protesting Piglet a bath. And what is the final result of Rabbit's plan to expel Kanga and Roo? The chapter ends: "So Kanga and Roo stayed in the Forest. And every Tuesday Roo spent the day with his great friend Rabbit."

Note the astonishing reversal in Rabbit's attitude. What happens when he has succeeded in the kidnap attempt? "Rabbit was playing with Baby Roo in his own house, and feeling more fond of him every minute." Roo has become Rabbit's great friend. Are we now looking at a New Rabbit?

Kanga as Demeter

All but the youngest readers of this incident must have noticed the striking parallel with the ancient Greek myth of Demeter and Persephone (Ceres and Proserpina to the Romans). When Hades kidnapped Persephone and carried her off to the Underworld, her mother, Demeter, goddess of earthly fruitfulness, in her anger, laid an embargo on every kind of vegetable growth. At last, a compromise was reached: Persephone would spend the winter with Hades in the Underworld; the rest of the year on earth with her mother. Earthly fruitfulness returned to normal.

Kanga, who represents fruitfulness in our texts, is an obvious symbol of Demeter. Roo enacts Persephone. We have already noticed enough examples of the reversal of traditional genders not to be surprised at this. Indeed, it is particularly appropriate to the theme of this chapter. Persephone's regular returns to her kidnapper in the Underworld are paralleled by Roo's regular Tuesdays with his kidnapper, Rabbit.

Can we, though, accept Rabbit as the representative of Hades, god of the Underworld? I agree that the analogy does not leap unbidden to the mind. A little reflection, however, soon persuades us that it is entirely appropriate. What, after all, are the chief characteristics of Hades? He was the god of the Underworld—to which his name is often extended—and he was a stern judge. Now, which of the Forest-dwellers lived underground? Rabbit, of course. This is powerfully emphasized in Pooh's early visit to Rabbit, and I have pointed out its function as a place of initiation (pages 167–169). Then, of all Pooh's friends, who was the most inclined to stern judgments? Rabbit. When Pooh gets stuck in Rabbit's doorway—" 'It all comes,' said Rabbit *sternly,* 'of eating too much' " (my emphasis). And it was Rabbit's stern sentence of exile against Kanga and Roo that led to the incident we are now exploring.

A final, clinching proof of the Kanga–Demeter link comes from the Greek Mysteries mentioned at the beginning of this chapter. Both, you will remember, were in honor of Demeter, and both involved the sacrifice of a pig or a piglet, possibly by drowning. Clearly Kanga's bathing the reluctant Piglet was lighthearted parody of this rite.

There are, of course, also striking differences. Whereas the anger of Demeter had disastrous effects, Kanga experienced only momentary alarm, and all the consequences were happy. Of all the special friendships that resulted from this potentially damaging incident, the most important was the special friendship between Kanga and Pooh. This friendship had already been prefigured when, just a few pages earlier, we read, "Pooh, who had decided to be a Kanga. . . ." This clearly indicates that close relationship between the female and male principles that is the theme of this chapter.

But what about Pooh's part in the kidnapping of Roo?

For most of this episode, Pooh's attitude is noticeably detached. When Rabbit is addressing him and Piglet at the beginning of the chapter, he does little but ask apparently irrelevant and even absurd questions. Rabbit is clearly irritated by these, and completely fails to take in Pooh's repeated hints that the whole plan is misguided.

Pooh does, however, cooperate to some extent. As in the case of the Heffalump Trap, he allows a misguided plan to proceed far enough to reveal its innate absurdity. He himself naturally acts primarily as a—doubtless amused—observer. It is significant that the poem he recites to distract Kanga's attention while Piglet jumps into her pouch is a collection of unanswered questions, hinting at a refusal to commit himself seriously to the present scheme. Particularly relevant to the theme of substitution and misidentification are the last two lines of the third stanza:

> *I sometimes wonder if it's true*
> *That who is what and what is who.*

The Mysterious Origins of Pooh and Kanga and the Special Connection Between Them

The first thing we are told about Kanga and Baby Roo is that "Nobody seemed to know where they came from."

This mysterious origin is, significantly, something she shares with Winnie-the-Pooh. When Piglet talks about his grandfather, Trespassers W, Pooh, you will remember, wonders what a grandfather is. "Grandfather" here is obviously representative of patriarchy, so this short passage shows us that patriarchy was no part of Pooh's psyche. It was not something he had rejected: It was something innately foreign to him.

In the opening paragraph of the chapter that introduces Kanga and Roo, we read that when Pooh asks Christopher Robin how these newcomers came, he answers,

> *"In the Usual Way, if you know what I mean, Pooh," and Pooh, who didn't, said "Oh!" Then he nodded his head twice and said, "In the Usual Way. Ah!"*

It is sad to have to admit that there still seem to be some readers who are inclined to think that Milne was recording real ignorance on Pooh's part. Of course, what Pooh *really* did not know was that Kanga and Roo had come in the Usual Way. Because, of course, they hadn't. His profound intuitive knowledge must have assured him that their Way was far from Usual. The special connection between Pooh and Kanga is seen on several occasions. They cooperate in getting Roo out of the river when he falls in during the Expotition to the

North Pole. Roo's first public appearance at a social function is his attendance at the party given in Pooh's honor. It is noteworthy that his first words on this occasion are, "Hallo, Pooh!" The Great Bear immediately acknowledges him with a "Hallo, Roo!" Again, we must remind ourselves that nothing in the Pooh myth is accidental. Even the most apparently conventional courtesy is fraught with meaning.

Tigger provides one of the most important examples of how Pooh and Kanga work together. It is Pooh who hospitably welcomes Tigger into the Forest. It is Kanga who "knew at once that, however big Tigger seemed to be, he wanted as much kindness as Roo." She demonstrated this kindness in practical terms. Tigger discovered that Roo's Extract of Malt is "what Tiggers like."

Which explains why he always lived at Kanga's house afterwards, and had Extract of Malt for breakfast, dinner, and tea. And sometimes, when Kanga thought he wanted strengthening, he had a spoonful or two of Roo's breakfast after meals as medicine.

By now, we have come to realize much more of Kanga's importance. We recognize her as an Earth Mother, a symbol of fertility. All this makes her a much more potent figure than has generally been understood.

Still, however, it leaves her in a stereotypically female role as carer and nourisher. And this applies equally to her role as preserver of order: "Kanga had felt rather motherly that morning, and Wanting to Count Things— like Roo's vests, and how many pieces of soap there were left." Her dealings with Tigger reveal a much more powerful aspect.

In our chapter on the tarot, I called attention to the card entitled "Strength," which shows a woman controlling a big cat, usually a lion. At that stage, it was enough to note the parallel with Kanga's easy control of the Bouncy Tigger. Now the time has come to explore further.

The great goddesses of the ancient world are often depicted with animals: bulls, snakes, doves and bees. Most of all, though, with the big cats, especially lions. A terra-cotta sculpture of about 6000 B.C. shows a mother goddess actually giving birth between two lions or leopards. Jumping to about 1600 B.C., there is a seal showing a goddess standing on a mountain, with a lion on each side. From the second century A.D., we have a Roman bronze statue of the mother goddess Cybele in her chariot drawn by two lions.

This small selection impresses us with the awesome power of a tradition spanning over six thousand years. Now we can begin to comprehend the true meaning of Kanga, and the specialness of her close friendship with Pooh. But there is still more to it than that.

A vase painting of about the fifth century B.C. depicts the goddess Artemis with—and clearly in control of—a lion. Now, Artemis, "Mistress of Wild Animals," was especially linked with *bears,* and may, in some early versions, herself have adopted the form of a bear. Certainly, the little girls who attended her were called her bears. In some later versions, one of her attendants, the nymph Callisto, was turned into a bear, and her son is turned into the constellation Ursa Major! Could there be more overwhelming evidence of a very special connection between Winnie-ther-Pooh and Kanga?

Yes, there could! And here it is. Though we know Artemis as a Greek goddess, her origin was not Greek at all. She came from the far north, from what the Greeks called the Land of the Hyperboreans: the land beyond the North Wind, that is, the North Polar regions.

There is yet more to convince the skeptic. We know Artemis chiefly as a virgin huntress. But she was also a goddess of childbirth. This is not as paradoxical as it may seem. For a virgin in the most ancient times did not necessarily mean a woman who had never had sex: It meant one who never acknowledged any male as her master. Significantly, we hear nothing of a mate for

Kanga or a father for Roo. Like many of the great fertility goddesses, she was self-sufficient.

Not only is the bear specially connected with Artemis, it is also the oldest sacred animal, regarded as such as early as about 75,000 B.C.* Moreover, and here is another striking similarity: The most ancient sacred bears were female. Perhaps the oldest depiction of maternal affection, as distinct from mere fertility, is a statue of a sacred mother bear cuddling her cub (*ca* 4500 B.C.). The ancient belief that the bear cub was born shapeless and literally licked into shape by its mother was not just a curious, and unfounded, tale. It was also a symbol of the shaping power of the sacred animal, or rather of the mother goddess the bear represented.

The Significance of Kanga as a Kangaroo

Remembering again that our researches into the mysterious and the remote must never let us overlook the evident and the near-at-hand, let us return from Kanga's symbolic links with Artemis and bears to the most obvious thing about her: She is a kangaroo.

---

* There is evidence of a Bear cult practiced by Neanderthal people before the end of the last Ice Age.

If any of my readers have not read D. H. Lawrence's poem "Kangaroo," I urge them to do so. It is one of his finest poems. In addition, it contains many passages that illuminate our understanding of Kanga. Resisting the temptation to quote at length, I will concentrate on a few of the most strikingly relevant lines.

Delicate mother Kangaroo
Sitting up there rabbit-wise, but huge, plumb-
      weighted,
And lifting her beautiful slender face, oh! so much
      more gently and finely lined than a rabbit's, or
      than a hare's,

Coming to these lines fresh from our reading of Rabbit's initial hostility and final reconciliation with Kanga and Roo, we are bound to be struck by Lawrence's uncanny linking of them, both by comparison and contrast. Was Lawrence too an esoteric Ursinologist? The following lines do hint at this. He describes

. . . her big haunches
And, in addition, the great muscular python-stretch of
      her tail.

And again, her departure:

On the long flat skis of her legs,
Steered and propelled by that steel-strong snake of a
     tail.

These lines emphasize her strength as well as her beauty and gentleness. But her tail is not only "steel-strong," it has "python-stretch." The snake was one of the mightiest ancient symbols of wisdom and power, and the original Python was the dragon or serpent that guarded the shrine of the Oracle at Delphi. Moving on from these impressive—and, I think, previously unnoticed—Lawrentian references to Kanga, I come to the end of his poem:

Leap then, and come down on the line that draws to
     the earth's deep, heavy centre.

Leaping refers us back to the passages already mentioned, which tell us that Pooh had decided to be a Kanga, and about his jumping lessons. Two questions must suggest themselves to every reader. How do we interpret this astonishing reversal of conventional roles by which Kanga becomes the teacher and Pooh the pupil? Second, why did Pooh want to learn to jump?

One answer to the first question might be that

even the greatest sage might need tuition in some purely technical matter of no great importance. Jumping might be considered just such a matter. I am confident my readers will intuitively reject this plausible but shallow solution. And they will be right.

Many times, and with reference to many different kinds of esoteric path, we have seen Winnie-the-Pooh illustrating the age-old urge to rise above earthly limits. Great though his successes were, all involved external aids: the tree, the balloon or the staircase. Kanga's mighty leaps symbolized a way of transcendance without external aids, solely by the use of her own innate powers. Like a true Magus, Pooh combined the wisdom to recognize his existing limitations, the confidence to break through them, and the humility to learn from another. So we see the answers to both our questions, and we can better understand and more enthusiastically admire the free cooperation of Pooh Bear and Kanga.

Now let us look again at the last line of Lawrence's poem, focusing on the second part. This tells us that after leaping, the Kangaroo comes "down on the line that draws to the earth's deep, heavy centre."

This is the final clue we needed to answer the question posed in the first words of the chapter we have been considering: "Nobody seemed to know where they came from, but there they were in the Forest." Kanga herself knew, of course, and so did Pooh. His question about it to Christopher Robin was not a request for information but an examiner's question to a candidate; a test which Christopher Robin once again failed to answer correctly, or even to understand.

I have just said that Lawrence's poem supplied the last clue to this mystery. I will now tabulate the others. As we shall see, this evidence will not only solve our immediate problem, it will also throw light on many remaining obscurities. To enable my readers to follow the chain of evidence themselves, as easily as possible, I give references to each clue. To avoid long-winded rep-

etition, I adopt the common scholarly convention of abbreviating the titles and chapter numbers, thus: wp. 3 for *Winnie-the-Pooh*, Chapter Three; hpc. 1 for *The House At Pooh Corner*, Chapter One. Examining these clues, we find:

1. Winnie-the-Pooh is clearly and consistently pictured as a Brown Bear. Yet when Christopher Robin visits him in the Zoo, he "goes to where the *Polar* Bears are" (my emphasis). (wp. Introduction)
2. Much though Pooh enjoys the sun, he seems equally happy in snow. He goes Woozle-hunting in the snow (wp. 3). His love of snow is still more strongly expressed in his "special Outdoor Song which Has To Be Sung In The Snow." (hpc. 1)
3. He finds the North Pole. Note that both Kanga and little Roo play significant roles in this Expotition. (wp. 8)
4. When Pooh asks him about other Poles, Christopher Robin tells him there is a South Pole, "and I expect there's an East Pole and a West Pole, though people don't like talking about them." (wp. 9)
5. "Pooh went out to discover the East Pole by himself." (wp. 9)
6. Pooh dreamt "He was at the East Pole, and it was a very cold pole with the coldest sort of snow and ice all over it." (wp. 9)

7. Kanga, among other things, represents Artemis, who came originally from the land of the Hyperboreans, the North Polar regions. Yet as a kangaroo, she comes from the southern hemisphere. Lawrence's Kangaroo is explicitly "antipodal."

8. Kanga came down on "the line that draws to the earth's deep, heavy centre."

Putting all this together, we are irresistibly led to the following conclusions: The first three clues establish a special affinity between Pooh and the Polar regions. The third associates Kanga also with the North Pole, and this association is strongly reinforced by her symbolic role as an Artemis-figure (clue seven). The superficial contradiction between this and her antipodal function is reconciled when we think clearly about "the line that draws to the earth's deep, heavy centre." Surely even the most skeptical must agree that this line is the axis joining the two Poles: a superb symbol of that union of opposites that is an essential feature of so many esoteric systems.

Before revealing yet another esoteric level of the World of Pooh, I must answer a question which must be in my readers' minds: What about clues four through six? Especially, what about Pooh and the East Pole?

The Earth's Axis

A glance at even the smallest terrestrial globe shows
that the earth's axis is not perpendicular but is tilted at
an angle of 23.5 degrees. Many authorities inform us
that the axis was once perpendicular. The question of
when and how this changed is far too vast to consider
now. Suffice it here to record the theory of that original
but somewhat eccentric French philosopher Charles
Fourier (1772–1837), the theory that the earth had un-
dergone a very dramatic shift of over ninety degrees.
According to Fourier, the present North Pole started
due west, and gradually swung east to its present position. Originally, therefore, the North Pole was in a temperate climate, while the present eastern lands were as
cold as the present North Pole. So now we can understand that Pooh's dream of an icy East Pole was either
what philosophers call a thought experiment to test
Fourier's theory, or—a more intriguing idea—a memory from his own remote past.

Fascinating though these speculations are, they
may seem to belong more to cosmology than to the
Ancient Mysteries. These are not entirely separate, for
many explain the widespread myths of a former Golden
Age, an earthly Paradise, the Garden of Eden, as vague
but powerful memories of a time when a perpendicular
axis gave a more equable climate. In its own way, the

World of Pooh illustrates the lasting power of this myth.
Now, however, I am more concerned with the mystical
rather than the physical importance of the earth's axis.
This concern inevitably leads to another earthly paradise, the World of Shambhala.

Another Dimension: Is the World of Pooh Shambhala?

Having clarified the ancient concept of some kind of
Polar connection between earth and heaven, and the
idea of a perpendicular earth's axis, we can now consider the belief, well known in esoteric circles, in two
mysterious "places," Shambhala and Agartha. Both
names have variant spellings. Nor is it only their names
which vary. Different occultists situate them as far apart
as the Himalayas, the Gobi Desert, and even South
America.

The whole story is too long and complicated to examine here. The essentials are the belief that the original North Pole was an earthly paradise, both spiritually
and materially. When the earth's axis shifted, the spiritual center shifted also. Where it shifted *to* is, as I have
said, a matter of dispute. Two other matters are also in
dispute. Some Polarists—a common name for the be-
lievers in some kind of mystical value in the Polar regions—believe that there was an evil underside to this
paradise. To confuse matters further—oh, for the clarity

of *our* author's text!—some call the paradisal state Shambhala and the evil Agartha; others reverse the names.

Readers may have noticed the quotation marks enclosing the word "places" above. This alludes to another controversy. Three different beliefs have their adherents. 1. Shambhala is a physical place with a geographical location, however hidden. 2. It is purely a state of mind, to be reached by meditation and other mental disciplines. 3. It is a mental state but one associated with some kind of actual place.

On both the choice of name and the nature of Shambhala, I am content to be guided by the authority of the present Dalai Lama, who stated that "even though Shambhala is an actual land—an actual pure land—it is not immediately approachable by ordinary persons such as by buying an airplane ticket." What could be stronger confirmation of earlier hints that the World of Pooh is the most satisfying embodiment of the earthly paradise ever presented? What could be a more superb description of this World: "an actual land," but not to be reached by any ordinary, material form of travel?

Axis and Temple in the Ancient World

We now return from these somewhat speculative regions to solidly based history. Many ancient peoples believed that the earth's axis was, in some way, prolonged to the limits of the universe. Many ancient temples were sited on what the builders believed to be the earthly extremity of this axis. Temples of this sort aimed at producing—in the geometrical sense of the word—the line of the axis so as to connect earth with heaven. The temple at Nippur in Babylonia was called Dur-an-ki, the Bond of Heaven and Earth. The most spectacular examples were the ziggurats of ancient Sumeria in the third millennium B.C. These consisted of a kind of stepped pyramid, which worshippers could ascend. The Tower of Babel was probably based on some such temple, as seen through hostile Hebrew eyes.

This may seem remote from the World of Pooh, which is completely lacking in large-scale architecture. We must remember, though, the one piece of building we do find in it: the house that Pooh and Piglet built for Eeyore. A first glance at Shepard's illustration of this house (see page 186) will hardly suggest a ziggurat to the uninstructed eye. Happily, our eyes are not uninstructed. We know historically these mighty temples descended from a long line of far simpler structures. Baring and Cashford inform us in their magnificent *The Myth of the Goddess,* "The temple evolved from the cow-byre and the sheepfold." So we are in no way straining credibility when we point to Shepard's picture as visibly showing an early form, which to us implies its future development.

We are confirmed in our interpretation by the leading participants in this incident. The builders are the Great Bear and his chosen disciple, Piglet. The beneficiary is Eeyore. He, as we saw in the chapter on the tarot, is the Questor. By installing him in this proto-ziggurat, they are symbolically starting him on the ascent to the Higher Planes.

The Others

In the last few pages, we have been focusing on Pooh and Kanga, not forgetting Roo. Pooh's other friends also have a bearing on the Female Mysteries. Piglet not only helps to build the proto-ziggurat, he reminds us of the pig-goddesses of the ancient Middle East. Tigger as symbolic lion has been present again and again.

Though we tend to see Owl as the quintessential bachelor don, typically resenting any female's attempts to tidy his study, yet we must not forget that the owl was traditionally associated with many ancient goddesses. The four-thousand-year-old relief of the Sumerian goddess Inanna-Ishtar shows her with two owls as well as two lions, and we are familiar with the owl as the companion of Pallas Athene, Goddess of Wisdom. Those powers I have repeatedly felt guiding me on this journey obviously inspired Shepard when he drew his picture of Owl flying over the waters during "the Terrible

Flood," a picture known to those whose deeper researches have led them to the colored edition of *Winnie-the-Pooh*. This picture unquestionably refers to the Neolithic Bird Goddess, who often flew above the waters in the shape of an owl.

We have already noticed the revolution in Rabbit's attitude, to a more nurturing role. No doubt readers have also noted the repeated emphasis on Rabbit's numerous and remarkably varied friends-and-relations. Surely a plain symbol of fertility, one which fits the proverbial fertility of rabbits. Eeyore too shows a caring attitude in his attempts to rescue Roo by hanging his tail in the water, and his joining in the Search for Small. True, his efforts are misapplied, but his goodwill is beyond doubt. He deserves his reward as he is given the place of honor when the Farewell to Christopher Robin is organized.

If any readers feel that I have at any moment digressed from the subject of the Female Mysteries, I would remind them that this chapter is arguing against all rigidly confining gender roles. And I am doing this by emphasizing the close similarities, indeed the quasi-identity of Pooh and Kanga. Just as we must recognize the majestic power—and even the potential ferocity—of Kanga, so we must recognize the caring and nurturing element in Winnie-ther-Pooh. Everyone in the World of Pooh, however, shares, if indirectly, in the recognition of the Female Mysteries and their modern equivalent: the breakdown of rigid gender roles.

Nor must we forget that it was an examination of the Female Mysteries that cast light on Pooh and Kanga's mysterious origins and allowed us to see the full significance of the World of Pooh as an Enchanted Place.

What could be a more fitting climax to this brief introduction to the occult wisdom of the Great Bear?

Conclusion

Now we have come full circle. Starting with the Great Bear in the Polar sky, we end with the Polar myth of Shambhala. It was while gazing at the northern night sky that the esoteric significance of Winnie-ther-Pooh was first revealed to me. I can hardly doubt this revelation was the work of the Higher Planes or that it guided me along the path my readers and I have travelled together.

That Path unfolded with irresistible logic. The double significance of the Great Bear, as constellation and as Pooh Bear, showed us the profound astrological meaning of those texts we had so often enjoyed but so little understood. Astrology inevitably led to alchemy, both of which were traditionally combined in the Hermetic philosophy.

Study of the tarot not only enlarged our knowledge of the Enormous Brain of Pooh, but also enriched our appreciation of his companions; especially, perhaps, of Eeyore. The endpapers clearly pointed to Pooh as a Druid, and his role as a Bear of the Trees must appeal strongly to all of us today who are concerned about the environment.

The continuing vitality of the Pooh cycle obviously parallels the even longer vitality of Arthurian legend. It also gives a more dignified position to Christopher Robin, as Arthur to Pooh's Merlin. Pooh's function as guide is further developed as we see him leading his companions as far as their natures permit along the Path to Enlightenment: a process in which Piglet is the most spectacular triumph.

The Qabalah reveals Winnie-ther-Pooh as a master of that supreme Ancient Mystery. Its system of numerology confirms many of our previous intuitions, and also solves several puzzles, especially concerning Owl.

By the time we reach the last chapter, we have been well prepared for that most astonishing revelation of all: the revelation that the superficially masculine World of Pooh contained the profoundest Female Mysteries.

But we have, perhaps, come far enough to recognize the World of Pooh as a mythical world, equal in status to those other mythical worlds: Eden, the Golden

World, the Realm of Logres, Shambhala. It is not only a mythical world but also a *mystical* world, and like all such mystical worlds, the Way is both *through* and *to* them. The journey to them is itself an exploration of them. The title promised to reveal Winnie-ther-Pooh's profound knowledge of the Ancient Mysteries. The overwhelming mass of evidence made this an easy task. I also promised, however, to reveal him as the Supreme Magus of the Second Millennium. While many things throughout the book looked forward to this, it is perhaps the last chapter which most clearly points to our hopes for the next era. Under the guise of a children's tale, we have a model of personal relations and of society.